Starting A Business

By the same author

Managing Your Company's Finances
(with R.H. Smith)

STARTING A BUSINESS

A Practical Handbook with examples

- Planning
- Forecasting
- Raising Finance
- Tax and legal matters
- Controlling the business

Richard L. Hargreaves

BA(Cantab), MSc, PhD, ACIS

HEINEMANN : LONDON

Published in association with Newmarket Venture Capital Ltd

William Heinemann Ltd
10 Upper Grosvenor Street London W1X 9PA
LONDON MELBOURNE TORONTO
JOHANNESBURG AUCKLAND

First published 1983
© Richard L. Hargreaves 1983

434 90687 5

Typeset by Inforum Ltd, Portsmouth
Printed in Great Britain by
Redwood Burn Ltd, Trowbridge

This book is dedicated to Adele
because it is about beginnings.

Contents

Preface xi

1 FIRST THOUGHTS 1
Introduction
Reasons for Owning a Business
Advantages of Your Own Business
Disadvantages of Your Own Business
Should you Take the Plunge?
Planning and Outside Help

2 COMMON BUSINESS START-UPS 6
Introduction
The Small Retailer
The Existing Work Skills Business
The Own Invention Business
The Purchased Franchise
The Quick In-out
The Purchased Business
The Management Buy-out
Making Your Choice

3 BUSINESS PLANNING 14
Introduction
Planning Guidelines
Your Business Plan
The Market
Competition
Customers
Products
Patents
Production

Pricing
Suppliers
Premises
Plant and Equipment
Partners and Staff
Working Capital
Investors
Summary

4 PROFIT AND CASH FORECASTING   34
Introduction
What are Cash Flow, Profit and a Balance Sheet?
Assumptions for the Forecasts
Period of the Forecasts
Forecasting Profit
Forecasting Cash Flow
Forecasting Balance Sheets
Other Matters
Summary

5 FINANCIAL NEEDS   63
Introduction
Minimizing your Finance Needs
The Financial Structure of Your Business
Types of Finance
Outside Finance

6 SEEKING FINANCE   74
Introduction
Sources of Finance
Making an Application
What the Financier Wants
What you Should Look For From a Financier
Summary

7 LEGAL AND TAX MATTERS   96
Introduction
Partnership or Limited Company?
The Legal Side of a Partnership
The Legal Side of Incorporation
General Comments on Tax
Partnership Taxation
Limited Company Taxation
Formal Registration Requirements
Employing People

8 CONTROLLING YOUR BUSINESS   119
  Introduction
  Minimum Records to Keep
  Minimum Control Information
  Budgeting
  Management Accounts
  Credit Control
  Surviving a Cash Crisis
  People

9 SUCCESS OR FAILURE?   144
  General Comments
  Increasing your Chance of Success
  Avoiding Failure
  Summary

10 OUTSIDE HELP   151
  Introduction
  Contacts
  Accountants
  Solicitors
  Banks and Investing Institutions
  Official Bodies
  Consultants
  Others

11 GETTING BIGGER   156
  Introduction
  Planning and Control
  Delegation and an Organization
  People
  Outside Finance

APPENDICES
  1 Explanations of Technical Terms   161
  2 Sources of Help   169
  3 The Newmarket Group   179
    Reading List   185

    List of Examples   187
    Index   191

Acknowledgements

If this book achieves its aim of being helpful to the person who is thinking about starting his own business, it is partly due to the help I have had from a number of people particularly my former colleagues at ICFC. I would like to record my appreciation of the specific help given by the following:

Nigel Lewis, who has run his own business; Julian Burnett, who might one day be tempted to do so and Chris Tanner, who is financial director of a small business, all of whom read and criticised the text in draft form.

Anthony Lewis, a practising solicitor, who criticised the legal references and Nick Green who checked the arithmetic.

Derry Vaughan and Sue Price who typed and retyped the manuscript.

Richard Hargreaves

Preface

Over recent years small and new businesses have become fashionable. Everybody seems to want either to start them, finance them or encourage their existence. In addition, recession has encouraged existing companies to slim down, lay off staff and sell spare activities. All of this produces great opportunity and stimulus for the budding entrepreneur. However, the other side of the coin is that any new business needs considerable planning and will involve very real business and personal risks. So any decision to go ahead needs to be taken with care.

This book is an attempt to help the intending new businessman both with his decision to go ahead or not and with his business planning. It is essential that starting your own business is approached with thoroughness and a full recognition of the risks involved. Some people are so attracted to the possibility of success and wealth that they are careless and take personal risks which result in tragedy. It is hoped that this book will help you to avoid this trap. At the other extreme there are those who perhaps sit at a desk in a large company feeling frustrated and are full of bright ideas to start in business but overwhelmed by the thought of how to go about it. It is hoped this book will serve to encourage such people to take the plunge by helping them put the risks and problems into perspective.

The book takes a practical approach to all of the topics a new businessman needs to consider. This includes how to decide on the amount of finance reqired and how to raise it. Finance for start-ups is now available from many sources including banks, institutions and private individuals. If you can put together a sensible business plan, find a little money personally and approach the right financier you will be able to raise money more easily than has been possible for many years.

Careful preparation and planning coupled with adequate finance should ensure a successful birth of the new business. Its future will depend, however, on proper management control. This needs good accounting information which is available frequently and promptly. Initial control systems may be simple but are vital if the business is not to fail in its early, fragile days. Finally, therefore, the book deals briefly with some of these problems.

The approach adopted is a practical one with lots of checklists and guidance points. It is assumed, however, that a thorough business plan will be required. Some of this detail is not necessary for the simplest type of start-up such as, for example, a small retail shop. As a result the text is principally aimed at those who wish to start a more complex or larger business.

R.L. Hargreaves

1

First Thoughts

Introduction

Many people think about running a business of their own at some time in their life. With some this is no more than day-dreaming. Others are more serious. This book is written for those who are serious about the idea of their own business but wish to think about matters fully before committing themselves. It is also, hopefully, of interest to those who have already decided to go ahead but want some help with their detailed planning.

This first chapter sets the scene for the rest of the book. It aims to take you through the preliminary thinking you need to do even before you start detailed planning. This includes looking at the advantages and disadvantages of owning your own business and carefully examining your motives before committing yourself. If you do this properly you will have a good idea of what you might be letting yourself in for.

Reasons for Owning a Business

Few businesses succeed without problems, considerable hard work and great determination. Many businesses fail, causing their owners disappointment, loss of money, and possible bankruptcy. It therefore makes sense to examine closely your motives for wanting to own a business. If they are only a whim or a reaction to a particular set of circumstances your chances of success are limited. It is important that your decision remains constant even when the going gets tough – as it sometimes will.

No two budding entrepreneurs are likely to have quite the same reasons for their decision to start a business. Once the decision is taken and the commitment made, the reasons are not of great importance. However, if you are still considering whether to take the plunge, it is worth noting some common reasons why others have done it.

Some reasons are a reaction to circumstances. A common one is frustration at work. This may be due to a failure to obtain promotion. It may be a dislike of the way the company is run or the people who run it. Or it may be an inability to get ideas, or inventions, adopted. In short, the individual believes either that he is not being given credit for his ability or that he can do it better than his employers.

Unfortunately, redundancy is frequently the occurrence which stimulates action. It does have the advantage that the loss of a career is not at stake – it having already been lost – and that some finance may be available from a redundancy payment. Other reasons come from a desire for independence or the wish to make money. To the outsider it might seem that making money is always the driving force behind any entrepreneur but this is often not so. Certainly such people expect to make money but the fun of independent decisions and achievements are more important to many. Indeed, planning for expansion and the achievement of a steadily growing profit record is often wanted as much for the excitement of the game as the additional financial rewards that may result.

Advantages of Your Own Business

Some of the advantages of your own business are obvious. There is the opportunity to make more money than is normally possible as an employee. This can mean extra salary and benefits whilst running the business. It can also mean the chance of a large profit if the business is sold.

The attraction of money is strong. However, for many people the freedom that comes from being their own masters is at least as important. This freedom includes no interference from others with day-to-day decisions. Also, and possibly more importantly, it gives the opportunity to control the longer-term direction of working life. To achieve both these freedoms as an employee is rare, although some occupations allow one of them. For example, an academic has considerable choice of direction in the studies which form much of his working life.

Despite a real increase in freedom, restrictions will remain because a business can only operate within society. On the one hand this involves the same moral considerations as for any other person in the society. On the other, there are official regulations which affect almost all aspects of business life. These range from taxation on profits, which sometimes seems to dominate business thinking, to control over environmental factors such as pollution control or planning permission for factory extensions.

Another advantage can be favourable tax treatment. This is true for the self-employed person who is permitted more allowances against income than an employee. Directors of companies owned by themselves are not self-employed for tax purposes but they usually take more benefits in kind (without paying the tax that equivalent amounts of salary would involve) than is common

2

for an employee. For example, hotel proprietors often live and eat in their hotels at little cost to their taxed income.

Finally, there may be specific government incentives to encourage business activities in certain geographical areas or industries. These include rent-free periods, interest relief grants, capital equipment grants and cheap money.

Disadvantages of Your Own Business

The attractions of your own business are considerable. Unfortunately, so are the drawbacks. They are so great that many who like the idea of running their own business still prefer to remain as employees.

Probably the greatest disadvantage is the lack of security compared with a safe job in a sound organization. Starting your own business sacrifices this and all its aspects including your pension rights. However, it should not be forgotten that even large employers can fail and loss of their jobs, through redundancy for example, is a risk all employees take. Thus job security may not be all it seems to be. Nevertheless, it is normally much greater as an employee of a large, well-established organization than as the owner of a small, new business.

To make matters worse, the owner of a small business risks more than unemployment if his business fails. At best he will have lost all he has worked hard for. However, further financial hardships may follow because, for example, of personal guarantees given to a bank to secure the business overdraft. This may lead to the sale of all his assets, particularly his private house which is probably his only real wealth. At worst bankruptcy will result. Then, as he tries to get back on his feet, he may find difficulty in getting a new job. He may have to accept a lower salary than he would like with limited pension prospects. These are real risks for most small businessmen and should not be accepted lightly.

Finally, the stress of running your own business is a disadvantage often overlooked. Considerable pressure and long hours of work are common for any entrepreneur. The stress is made worse for the owner of a small business who must make his decisions alone. He does not often have others of his intellectual calibre in the business with whom to discuss major decisions and a common failing is that he does not seek outside advice. At the least this can lead to a sense of isolation and a feeling of loneliness. At worst the stress can produce the loss of friends, a broken marriage, ill health and the failure of the business.

Should You Take the Plunge?

The risks involved in starting a business are real and should not be taken casually. In Great Britain some nine out of ten companies formed are subsequently struck off the register. The actual failure rate is less than this as some companies are never traded. However, it is still high and you should not forget this even though no-one believes it is his business which will fail. For some people the urge to start a business is so strong that there is never any question of not going ahead despite the risks. Before taking the plunge, however, most people need to give careful consideration to several key questions. These include:

1 Do the reasons for wanting to start a business stand up to examination?

It is wise to discuss the reasons with other people who are not emotionally involved with the plan. If they do not stand up to some criticism they may be unsound.

2 What would the price of failure be?

A proper answer depends on detailed budgeting of your financial requirements. The important point is not how much money might be lost but whether you can afford to lose it. Savings invested in a business and then lost are one thing. Money borrowed and lost is another as the debt will remain and repayment may involve much hardship.

3 Have the preparations been made as thoroughly as possible?

Full preparations include detailed financial forecasts. The secret is to do all that is possible to prepare before handing in your notice and having to depend on the new business to pay your grocery bills and mortgage. While planning is vital to maximize the chances of success, it does not directly produce income.

4 Can the risks be minimized?

Recognition of the risks is important to all business decisions. All such decisions involve risk and, in general, the greater the chance of profit the greater the risks involved. Only when risks are recognized can sensible plans be made to minimize them. Some risks will inevitably remain but contingency plans can be made if early warning of failure is available. This is only possible if proper forecasts have been prepared against which to monitor progress.

The decision to proceed probably depends on whether you can afford to fail. Unfortunately, many people do not ask themselves this question because failure is something that happens to somebody else. The concept of risk is often hard for the potential businessman to grasp, yet it is a key factor in the decisions to be taken in starting and running any business. The final decision to go ahead is a very personal one but it cannot be emphasized too strongly how valuable it is to have considered all the aspects of that decision if the chance of tragedy is to be minimized and the chance of success enhanced.

5 Will I get support from my spouse and family?

You should not overlook the importance of your family in deciding to go it alone. Your spouse will have to suffer the stress with you but may not fully appreciate the excitement you will also have. The long hours, worry and possible loss of interest in other things may put a great strain on your marriage and family life. This can lead to tragedy. On the other hand, support from your family can be a great psychological help when things get tough.

Finally, remember that if you give a personal guarantee and, say, a second mortgage on the family home you should have the agreement of your spouse whose assets you are also risking.

Planning and Outside Help

The best way to minimize the risks involved in starting a business is to prepare thoroughly. This includes producing detailed business plans and reducing uncertainties to a minimum. Unfortunately, the commonest weakness of many existing small businesses is a failure either to plan properly or have effective means of financial control. To learn these disciplines from the outset is probably the best way of ensuring success. Careful preparation is so important that it is the central theme of this book.

Planning for a new business is not easy. For example, the key to any forecast of profit or cash is the sales performance which is exceptionally hard to predict for a new business. Yet as your business will fail if it runs out of cash, a forecast of the cash position – broken down into short periods of time to enable actual results to be compared with forecast – is a vital part of the overall planning. Also, the preparation of this forecast is the only way to decide how much finance you will need. Unless sufficient finance is available you should not go ahead and unless your plans are made properly it is not possible to know how much is required.

Once your plans are reasonably well advanced it is a good idea to consult outside professionals. People who can help include accountants, solicitors, bank managers and fellow small businessmen. Such professionals have experience of many of the matters you will be considering for the first time. They also are useful critics because they can stand back from your emotional involvement with the project. Unfortunately, not all professionals are good at giving the necessary advice and the existence of a professional qualification certainly does not guarantee it. Probably the best way to find a good adviser is by personal recommendation from another businessman. Also, it is false economy to use someone just because his rates are cheap. As with most things quality and cheapness do not usually go together.

2

Common Business Start-ups

Introduction

This chapter gives brief details of the commonest types of businesses which people start. It is a guide to the obvious possibilities for those who want to run their own business but are still deciding in which direction to go.

The Small Retailer

This is typically a small and family-run shop, hotel, pub or restaurant. It normally makes a living for the owner rather than making his fortune. It has limited growth potential unless other similar businesses are acquired or opened. It involves little or no processing of the purchased supplies. Almost all sales are for cash rather than credit. It is possibly the simplest kind of business which has an expectation of both long life and a steady but modest level of profit.

An example is the freehold pub bought by a retired couple for £75,000. They raised £30,000 of their own cash and a £15,000 interest-free loan from a brewery, and borrowed £30,000 over ten years from a bank which took a mortgage on the premises. The business makes them a good living and will remain readily saleable.

Its advantages are:

1 It is simple to run.
2 Relatively small amounts of money are needed if the premises are not freehold.
3 Sales are mainly for cash.
4 The prospects are steady if the products are not too fashionable.
5 The going business is readily saleable.
6 No particular skills are necessary to do reasonably well.

Its disadvantages are:

1 It is unlikely to make a lot of money (although a chain or a highly fashionable restaurant or night club might).
2 The small staff means holiday problems for the owner.
3 It will always be hard work unless you can afford to employ a manager.
4 It is vulnerable to drastic changes in its immediate environment such as the opening of a supermarket near to a small shop.

The Existing Work-Skills Business

This is one of the commonest forms of start-up. It might be a skilled toolmaker purchasing a lathe and starting up part time in a garage. Again, it might be the employed professional such as an accountant, estate agent, surveyor or architect who leaves his employer to go it alone. Also common is the person who acquires an activity or product from an employer who has lost interest in it. A small scale start makes many activities viable which would not be for a large company with large overheads.

The category includes many differing activities and types of business but it is common to have the possibility of real growth. Some of the most successful companies have started in this way.

An example is the three recruitment specialists who decided to go it alone in an unexploited area. They needed £40,000 of which they could raise £5,000 in cash. They raised the rest by personally guaranteeing a £15,000 overdraft and £20,000 came from an institution as £2,500 for one third of the equity and a £17,500 long-term loan. By its sixth month the business was making £5,000 profit per month.

Its advantages are:

1 A detailed knowledge of the product or service is possessed from the start.
2 Real growth (and wealth) possibilities can exist.
3 If the opportunity has arisen through redundancy, the risks are less than if a successful career would otherwise have to end voluntarily.
4 If a product or specialized service is involved the development costs (and risks) may already have been incurred.

Its disadvantages are:

1 A detailed knowledge of the technical side may give a false sense of security. This confidence may close the entrepreneur's eyes to his lack of knowledge of the additional skills necessary to run a business successfully.
2 The product or service may not be as viable as a small company project as

it appears to the person who is close to, and enthusiastic about, its development.

The Own Invention Business

This is the classic start-up. Many major manufacturing companies were started by an individual with a new product invention. There is unlimited potential if the product is right but it must not only do what is claimed but meet customer needs or it will not sell. Lack of market awareness is a common problem with inventors. Not only must the market exist but also the company has to find a way to introduce potential customers to the new product. The other main problem is that not all inventors really want to run a business or are capable of doing so. Usually they are more likely to succeed when teamed with a good business-man.

An example is the engineer who designed a new domestic aid which is cheaper and better than the Japanese alternatives. Considerable attention was paid to clear instruction books and methods of marketing the product. Initially he subscribed £20,000 for ordinary shares with an institution providing £10,000 for shares (one third of the total) and a £50,000 loan. He had already spent two years developing the product. The new finance was used for tooling (which was supplied to subcontractors) and working capital. Initial sales were all made to one major retailer though others were on stream by the end of the second year. In the first year losses were £20,000, the second year saw a profit of £25,000 and he forecast a profit of £65,000 for his third year. Everyone was delighted with progress. He found no difficulty raising extra finance from his bankers as he went along. The institution had committed £100,000 in total by the end of the second year and was prepared to consider more as the need arose.

Its advantages are:

1 The potential may be enormous.
2 The business is based on something unique which can ensure success if the product is right for the market and developed continuously to remain so.
3 If the product is unique the profit margins can be large, making the financing of the business easier.

Its disadvantages are:

1 The invention may not satisfy a market need.
2 Inventors do not always make good managing directors.
3 Unforeseen development costs may cripple the project in the early stages.
4 The product must be kept up to date or others must be developed if early success is to continue.

The Purchased Franchise

This is a fast-growing type of business which has spread from America to this country over the last few years. In its simplest form it is a central operation which develops and markets a service or a product which is then sold through a large number of outlets. Instead of owning these outlets, the central company sells or rents the use of its name and product to an individual who benefits from the national advertising. This is franchising. Examples include Holiday Inn, Kentucky Fried Chicken and Dyno-Rod drain cleaning.

One example of a small franchise operation is the three redundant executives who purchased an instant print franchise offering a range of quick printing services to customers. They needed to find £25,000 of which £15,000 was for plant and premises and the remainder as an initial fee to the franchise company, who also subsequently received a 10% royalty on sales, some of which was to be spent on central marketing. The proprietors found £10,000 in cash (from their redundancy payments) and borrowed £15,000 over seven years from a bank. A profit of £8,000 before tax was made in the first year with a hope of making about £25,000 when the full potential was reached.

Its advantages are:

1 Guidance, training and help with financial control is usually available centrally.
2 The market is stimulated by central advertising and promotions.
3 An established product or service is provided.
4 With care, risks are limited.
5 The clearing banks have managers specializing in financing franchises.

Its disadvantages are:

1 The organization which will make most money is the central operation. It controls prices and margins.
2 Some purchased franchises are very expensive and if, for example, the location is badly chosen expensive failure may result which costs the central operation very little.
3 There is little scope for growth though more franchises can be acquired.
4 In many cases, the full independence of running a business is lacking as the central control may be similar to the employer-employee relationship.

The Quick In-Out

This category does not lead to an established and continuing business. It is based on heavily marketing some gimmicky or otherwise appealing idea which will have a limited life with a view to making a lot of money quickly. If such a short-lived product was rapidly followed by others a stable business might result, but often the ideas are one-off or short lived. Unfortunately not all such ventures are entirely legitimate, the chance to make easy money being tempting to the less reputable investor.

One example is the lady who, some years ago, spotted the novelty of plastic balloon-blowing material sold in tubes by Far East manufacturers. She bought a number and sold them like hot cakes at three times their cost price by offering them from an ice cream seller's tray at two exhibitions. This went so well she decided to make a real killing and ordered a very large quantity direct from the Far East in time for the Motor Show.

The delivery failed to arrive on the expected day as it had gone to the wrong destination. By the time it did arrive she had missed the exhibition and the goods were damaged and not insured. Instead of an enormous profit she was in danger of making a large loss. To cut her losses she had to employ small boys to help repackage the undamaged tubes and sell them cheaply from street corners.

Its advantages are:

1 The chance to make a lot of money quickly if successful.
2 One good idea and some money is all that is needed.

Its disadvantages are:

1 No real business emerges.
2 There is often considerable financial exposure as many such schemes depend on flooding products on to the market.
3 Because there are many disreputable people in this business, its reputation is not good.
4 It is hard to judge when the idea has run its course and large left-over stocks can absorb earlier profits.

The Purchased Business

Here it is not the business that is new but its owner. This means that the new owner has to have sufficient money to buy out the old one. He also must be able to value the business before he is able to negotiate a sensible price. Many of the risks of a start-up are avoided but, in their stead, the main risk is not really knowing the business and its weaknesses until after it has been bought. A purchase of business assets from a receiver or liquidator also falls into this category.

One example is the two entrepreneurs, one of whom had a small printing company and one £100,000. They found a run-down business in the printing industry owned by a large public company which had lost interest in it. They bought the company for £500,000 which was half the value of its net assets. However, it was making small losses. They put together a business plan and persuaded an institution that it could make £250,000 profit per year. Their plan included retaining the existing managing director. They raised £50,000 for equity (one third of the total) from an institution which also provided a £350,000 loan. They also persuaded a bank to provide a £100,000 overdraft facility for trading purposes. The business has done only modestly during recession. There were many problems but they are still hoping to achieve profits of £250,000 once the recession is over.

Its advantages are:

1 The business already exists with customers, staff and operating assets.
2 If the business has not been fully exploited due to the age, indifference or lack of competence of the previous owner, a lot of money can be made from growth.

Its disadvantages are:

1 The amount of money required to buy a good business will be high.
2 Inevitably, relatively little will be known of the details of the business and its good and bad points before the purchase. Many bad mistakes have been made even by major companies who have considerable investigating ability.
3 The staff who will be crucial to the continuing success of the business may not take kindly to the change of ownership.

The Management Buy-out

Recently many large companies have reviewed their industrial strategy and discovered smaller subsidiaries which do not really belong. A sale to the management is often then preferred to sale to a third party. This does mean that few people have the opportunity. Indeed, in many ways, that opportunity is unique because it combines the attractions of buying an existing business without the drawback of not knowing it in detail. Although a lot of money may be involved, the strength of the situation is such that it is often possible for the management to raise several times their own stake from investment sources and yet remain in control of the equity.

An example is the management team who were told that their specialized engineering company was to be sold as it no longer fitted into the industrial strategy of their foreign parent company. The parent company wanted £250,000 for the business. The directors bought it with £50,000 of personal cash plus

£200,000 raised from an institution. This was provided in the form of £25,000 for one third of the equity and £175,000 as redeemable preference shares. A new bank was persuaded, with the institution's help, to provide a £250,000 overdraft facility for the working capital previously provided by the parent company. The business trebled its profits in three years.

Its advantages are:

1 It is often a once in a lifetime opportunity to buy something good which is known in detail.
2 The detailed knowledge of the business and the existing ability to manage it remove most of the usual risks.
3 If the management are long serving the price asked will often be very reasonable particularly if the seller prefers to avoid an open market sale.
4 It is relatively easy to raise the money for the purchase and retain control of the share capital. Sometimes the vendor will agree to deferred purchase terms which reduces the initial finance required.

Its disadvantages are:

1 The company is likely to acquire high levels of borrowing as a result of the financing of the change of ownership. This can put the business at risk.
2 Group supporting services, such as accounting, may need to be replaced.
3 The management will be in a more exposed position than before.

Making Your Choice

If you are lucky an opportunity will occur which is so good that there is little question of not going ahead. The chance of a management buy-out is a good example. Again, somebody you know well and trust might offer you first refusal of his business on retirement. However, for most people the decision is not so clear cut and some element of choice is present. This choice has two aspects, namely choice of business venture and whether to go ahead or not. The two aspects cannot be completely separated as the quality of the opportunity is likely to be a major factor in your decision to go it alone.

The most important point to appreciate in choosing a new venture is that the risks of failure greatly increase the less you know about it. Most budding entreprenuers already have to cope with problems of management without the benefit of sufficient previous experience. If this is coupled with no experience of the industry and the products, the combination is almost certain to invite disaster. This point is discussed in Chapter 9 and needs to be strongly stressed. So try and find a venture which makes the most use of your existing knowledge. There will be gaps. Ideally you should consider filling them by recruiting others who possess the skills you do not. For example, an inventor usually needs a professional manager alongside him to be most likely to succeed.

If you are looking around for ideas without your previous work experience being an obvious pointer, you should be aware that some industries are less attractive than others. For example, in recent years the meat trade has been increasingly politically manipulated. This, plus over-capacity, has led to very slim profit margins and large numbers of company failures. To enter such an industry at the present time, even with experience of the trade, would seem foolhardy unless the opportunity is outstanding. Ideally, the industry chosen should be a growth one where competition will be less and profit margins higher. A declining industry, and there are a number in the UK, tends to have high competition, low profit margins and be of less interest to investors.

There is no doubt that the best way to succeed as a small businessman is to have a 'unique selling edge'. This means offering a product or a service which is better than, or has the edge on, the competition. This feature does not have to be very spectacular. For example, guarantee of delivery by a particular date in an industry which is suspect in this area can command a premium price. Part of the success of organizations such as Securicor is just this. Again, extra quality or reliability can command high price premiums.

If the feature of the business which appeals to the customer is sufficiently unique and attractive, he will not be very sensitive to price. Nobody buys a Rolls Royce because it is cheap. That car is sold to people who want it so much for the quality or status that price is almost irrelevant to them. Thus high margins of profit can be achieved and competition is not to be feared provided the desirability of the product is maintained. Not only do most successful small businesses have some aspect of their products or services which sets them apart but a small business is often better able to offer special features than a large business because of greater flexibility. Also, the more specialized product may not appeal to large sectors of the market which leaves the field clear from big company competition.

In conclusion, you should look to building a company which in some way provides what others do not. You should aim to satisfy a clear market need within what is probably a small segment of a much bigger market. This does have the initial drawback that although the produce will sell at a high profit to the right customer, such customers may be hard to locate because they are few. However, once found they are likely to remain loyal provided their needs continue to be satisfied. This also leads to a conclusion that may not have seemed obvious at first, namely that marketing is important to the small company. Ironically, the better its products the more important marketing may be, if those who would buy its products are to be found in sufficient number.

3

Business Planning

Introduction

This chapter discusses the planning you will need to do before starting your new business. It will need to be done with great care if your chances of success are to be maximized.

The objective of the chapter is to help you approach your planning in a systematic way. First of all, you are urged to recognize the constraints which will affect you. These may include shortage of finance, lack of availability of skilled staff or an unwillingness to take a risk which may result in the family home being sold if you fail. Once identified these constraints will form a set of guidelines within which you will be free to plan. The key stage is then to decide on both your personal objectives and the objectives of the business. Many small companies do not appreciate the need to have specific objectives but without them proper planning is not possible. Finally, the chapter considers the various features of a business (products, customers, staff etc.) in turn to help you make decisions about each within the context of your objectives. Much of the difficulty of preparing your plan will arise from the way these separate decisions will interrelate – you will find that no decision can be made in isolation.

Before your planning is complete you will need to prepare detailed forecasts of sales, profit and cash. These will be an essential part of the plan. They will help to validate your plan (e.g. does the plan work within the finance available?) and will serve as a basis for monitoring future performance of the new business. Forecasts are discussed in the next chapter.

The chapter assumes that you have decided to go ahead and that it is only the details of how to proceed that need to be considered. Nevertheless, the actual planning process itself may prove an essential element in many people's decision to go ahead. For example, you may need to see if you can keep the finance needed within certain limits before it is possible to make a positive decision.

Planning Guidelines

Unfortunately, there will be constraints affecting any group of individuals who wish to start a business. These may include limited finance, lack of housing mobility and limits to the risks that can be taken for family reasons. You will need to carefully consider all of these as a preliminary to preparing your detailed business plan which must, of course, operate within them. If you do not prepare a plan this may mean that some constraints (e.g. the degree of personal financial risk which is to be accepted) are accidentally broken once the business starts because the consequence of certain decisions was not foreseen.

Table 3.1: Possible Constraints on a New Business Plan

---

1 FINANCE

Own

How much cash do the partners have?
How much can they borrow?
Are there friends or relatives who will help out on favourable terms?

Outsiders

What are the possible sources of outside finance?
How much, approximately, can be raised from a bank?
How much more, approximately, could be raised from an equity-taking source?

2 GENERAL

Are there locational restrictions?
Are there family views that need to be taken into account?
Do contracts with a previous employer impose restrictions?
Are there essential skills (e.g. financial) not covered by the partners?
Can other skilled staff be recruited?

3 RISKS

Financial

What level of risk are the partners prepared to take?
How much money can they afford to lose?
How much borrowings can they risk taking knowing they will have to repay them even if the business fails?
What are the consequences of business failure for future earning potential?

General

How trustworthy and committed is each partner?
Does he have the skills for the job he must do?
Is there sufficient certainty on other aspects of the business to justify proceeding?
What degree of confidence is there that sales can be achieved at the time forecast, in the amount forecast, and at the margin forecast?

Planning Guidelines

It is strongly recommended that you list the constraints which will affect you. Table 3.1 gives a check list to help with this but does not cover all possibilities. Using this list as a guide, Table 3.2 is an example of a possible actual list which will now become guidelines for a detailed plan. The final plan must then, of course, be prepared without going outside these guidelines.

Financial Constraints

At the top of your list of constraints is likely to be limited finance. One of the first things to check in your early discussions about the business is how much money each partner can raise. As some, if not all, of this money is likely to be borrowed, you will need to consider each partner's borrowing ability. This subject is discussed in Chapter 6.

In the early stages the amount of personal finance is likely to be only approximately known but it is a useful guide to whether the business can be started without finance from outsiders. Assuming outside finance may be

---

Table 3.2: An Example of a List of Guidelines for a Proposed New Business

---

1 FINANCE

Own

  (a) The partners can raise £10,000 in cash (Jim £5,000, Joe £3,000, Bill £2,000).

  (b) Bill's Aunt Agatha might invest £2,500 without requiring income on it.

Outsiders

  (a) Borrowing money by giving charges on houses is not acceptable to families.

  (b) Maybe £5,000 can be raised from a bank without giving personal guarantees on the strength of a good business plan.

  (c) If required maybe a further £15,000 or more could be raised from a source which will subscribe for a minority equity stake.

2 WORKFORCE

  (a) Existing skills cover all important areas but for accountancy. An accountant will be needed to prepare monthly figures. He would not be needed full-time.

  (b) To begin with only five people will be required (1 secretary, 2 lathe operators, 1 driver, 1 bookkeeper). These can easily be recruited except for the bookkeeper.

3 LOCATION/PREMISES

  (a) Must be local.

  (b) 1,000 sq. ft. short lease may be hard to find.

4 TARGET PERFORMANCE

The plan must make sure that enough cash is generated by month 7 to pay reasonable salaries to the directors. This probably means achieving monthly sales of £50,000 by this time.

---

needed, or preferred, its availability and cost will need to be established. As a very rough guide, you can assume that at least an equal amount of outside finance to your stake should be easy to find. It is obvious that the more outside finance that you need, the less the chance of raising the money. Also, as the amount you raise increases, the higher the likely cost in terms of special conditions and shares in the business.

General Constraints

Other constraints on your plan are likely to include the location of the business, availability of premises and availability of staff. Any one of these can be of such great importance that the whole plan must reflect it. For instance, if you wish to have your business near to home but suitable premises and staff are not available, it may be necessary to consider moving house.

An important and often overlooked area is a contract with a previous employer which may restrict future activities. A formal, individually-tailored contract is not common but most employees have a general contract of employment which includes restrictions on their activities while employed and sometimes afterwards. This needs studying with care. While an employer is not legally permitted to impose restrictions which would prevent an ex-employee earning a livelihood, some restrictions can apply. Most important are the problems which can arise if you wish to obtain business from customers of your previous employer or use a process or product you have developed while employed by him. The area is a legal minefield and few individuals could afford legal action if an irate large ex-employer decided to attack them. The problems are worst if you are a director of the company as you than have specific legal duties and obligations which could invite litigation if breached. It is important to be extremely careful about approaching customers of an existing employer for business prior to actually leaving. The best advice that can be offered is that if there are any doubts, good legal advice should be taken at the earliest opportunity. A further difficulty can sometimes arise if finance is sought from outsiders before leaving your employer. Some financial sources may not be prepared to make formal offers of finance until resignations have been handed in. This is because of the danger of them being seen to attract individuals to leave their employment taking something with them which arguably belongs to the employer. This may leave you with a difficult decision which is, at worst, to resign before being completely sure of the necessary finance.

Risks

Risks can be thought of in two distinct categories. The first is the business risks which are taken by any commercial enterprise, particularly a new one. The second is the personal risks which entrepreneurs take when they commit themselves to a new business.

17

Business risks are the actual risks involved in a commercial project and will affect its chance of success or failure. They are very real and you need to constantly bear them in mind when preparing your plan. It is a sound principle to minimize risks wherever possible consistent with the business making the intended progress. If an examination of your ideas suggests that a very high level of risk is present it may be best not to go ahead unless you can revise the plan to reduce the level substantially. Also finance is likely to be much harder to find if risks are very high. Business risks are constantly referred to throughout this book because of their importance and many of the points made are summarized in Chapter 9.

Personal risks are a different matter because they relate to what the consequences of failure will be for the individuals involved. Table 3.3 gives a list of these. However carefully you have planned, you would be foolish not to examine the personal consequences of failure and to consider whether these consequences can be accepted. Bad planning and preparation often means that risks are taken which are not intended. Some of the personal consequences of failure are very unpleasant indeed. Bankruptcy, divorce and loss of friends are tragic events which have resulted for some businessmen. This is one of the main reasons for urging that you plan carefully and thoroughly.

There is a real risk involved in borrowing money linked to personal guarantees. If the business fails and money is still owed to the bank, a means of repayment must be found. If it has taken a second mortgage, the bank will, by legal right, have the power to sell your house to repay its loan. You must therefore consider whether the consequences of failure (however remote these may seem) are acceptable to you and your family who live in the house. This may not be so. If you wish to keep the risks sensibly limited, a simple rule of thumb is that no finance should be raised on personal security unless that money could

Table 3.3: Some Risks of Starting a New Business and their Possible Consequences

Possible Personal Risks	*Possible Consequences*
Cash may be lost	Other possible uses lost
Personally borrowed cash may be lost	Inability to repay. Bankruptcy
Personal security given to a financier	The family may lose its home
Long hours, worry and possible financial hardship	Health problems. Family difficulties
If the going gets hard the partners may fall out	Divorce. Loss of friends. Failure of the business
A good career may be sacrificed	Inability to obtain an equivalent career if the business fails
The previous employer may be upset at a loss of customers or products	Litigation and possible restrictions on future activities

be repaid over a reasonable period from earnings from subsequent employment in the event of failure. It should also be remembered that once personal security has been given to a bank, it can be hard to get it released. If you are lucky enough to have assets besides the family home, such as an investment property, the consequences of offering them as security are more likely to be acceptable.

Starting a business is a difficult matter full of stress and problems. Overcoming the problems can be very rewarding but not all people are suitable for such an isolated and unprotected role. You will need to consider carefully how you will cope. For example, an entrepreneur sometimes needs a high, and perhaps unjustified, level of confidence if he is not to give up when the going gets difficult. Also, if you do not like taking decisions without others to back you up you are unlikely to be capable of coping with the demands of your own business.

Again, many people are not aware of how much they depend on others in a big company environment. One example of this was a man who had started several small businesses for his large employer and decided to go it alone. He appeared to have an ideal background. Unfortunately, he was not aware how much he had previously depended on the support he had received from a large

Table 3.4: Business Plan Check List

Objectives	What are our personal objectives?
	What are the business objectives?
	Have these been considered properly?
	Are they specific enough to be practical?
The Market	Does it exist?
	How big is it?
	What share is aimed for?
	Can we research this ourselves or do we need help?
Competition	Who is it?
	On what basis are they serious competitors (e.g. price, quality, service)?
	How will it be fought?
Customers	Who will the first ones be?
	How firmly can they be persuaded to sign orders before we start?
	Can they pay the necessary price?
	* How much will they buy?
	* At what price?
	* What credit will they require?
	* What will initial sales be?
Products	Do they meet real customer needs (i.e. will there be a demand)?
	* Are they fully developed including the means of manufacture?

Table 3.4 (*Cont'd*)

Patents	Are they needed?
	* If so, what is the cost?
	* In what countries should they be registered?
	Do we need good professional advice?
Production	* Can production be subcontracted?
	* If not, what parts can be bought in?
	* What size must initial capacity be?
	Are there sufficient production skills in the business?
	* What are the costs of making the products?
Pricing	On what basis will pricing be done?
	* What is the gross margin?
	Do we have sufficient costing/pricing expertise?
	Or do we need advice?
Suppliers	Are adequate supplies easily available?
	What about quality?
	* Are prices acceptable?
	* What credit is available?
	Are other factors such as after sales service important?
Premises	* What size of premises are needed?
	Are suitable premises available in a convenient location?
	* What are rent/rates etc?
	Will a new company be an acceptable tenant?
Plant, Equipment	* How much is required?
	Is it readily available?
	* At what price?
	* Should some be leased/rented?
Staff	* How many will be needed?
	Are they available?
	* At what cost?
	Will professional advice be needed?
Working Capital	* How much will be required?
(See Chapter 4)	How much outside finance will be required?
	* Is there enough to allow for contingencies?
Forecasts (profit and Cash)	Is enough information available to forecast sensibly?
(See Chapter 4)	
	* What is the break even level of sales?
	* When will it be achieved?
	Do the forecasts stand up to criticism by advisers?
Investors	Is outside finance required?
(See Chapter 6)	How much?
	Who is a sensible investor?
	Who is not?
	Can the finance be raised?
	* At what price?

Note   All asterisked items directly affect the total amount of finance required.

---

organization. As a result, his approach was too casual and he made a number of classic mistakes resulting in disaster.

Finally, it is well recognized medically that, if a person has too many major changes in his life at one time, the stress levels are very great and will increase the chance of ill health. Starting a business is clearly a major change of circumstance. If this coincides, for example, with a divorce and a move of house the level of stress is a risk which must not be ignored.

Your Business Plan

The rest of this chapter briefly covers the main headings of a business plan about which decisions must be made before the numerical forecasts of profit and cash flow can be made. These are the subject of Chapter 4. Table 3.4 gives a summarized check list of the items to consider. They are discussed in the following sections.

Objectives

It is important to be clear on your objectives before you start planning. The plan will then be prepared to achieve them. Indeed a plan is, by definition, a programme of actions needed if certain objectives are to be achieved. Many people try to plan without clear objectives which leads to vagueness and lack of direction.

First, you must consider your personal objectives, aims or ambitions. These need to be as specific as possible and will have a profound effect on the shape that your business plan takes.

Secondly, and independently, you must consider what the corporate objectives are to be. These will, of course, be dictated by the personal objectives which you have already set. Unfortunately, many smaller companies do not have clearly stated corporate objectives or aims. Most large companies do and regard these as a background against which to plan for the future. To be useful such objectives need to be clear. For example, a 20% annual rate of growth of profit, rewarding careers for staff and a definition of areas of business activity. You will need to give very careful thought to your corporate objectives before preparing your business plan. All your objectives may require modification from time to time but they should be so fundamental to the business philosophy that changes are not likely to be frequent or dramatic.

Table 3.5 gives a simple example of three completely different personal objectives, each of which relates to a business planned to start in a similar way and with the same activity. The great difference between these starting points can be seen to lead to very different corporate objectives. This illustrates the importance of deciding on your objectives at the earliest possible stage. Possible consequences of the corporate objectives are also shown to emphasize the differences which may result in terms of how the business is organized and financed.

21

Table 3.5: Examples of Possible Objectives for Three Start-ups in the Same Business

	A	B	C
FOUNDERS PERSONAL AIMS	To get rich by selling the company as soon as possible. To make at least £1m personally.	To build and run a growth company.	To make a good living in a business which can be passed on to the next generation.
CORPORATE OBJECTIVES			
(a) *Business*	Start with specialized machine shop but diversify into the most profitable activities which can be found.	Start with specialized machine ship with aim to become one of the best five in the South East.	Run a specialized machine shop providing good, quick service to the local industry.
(b) *Growth Rate*	As fast as possible. Maximise profits.	20% compound per annum with emphasis on steady growth rather than speed.	Keep business to a maximum of ten employees.
(c) *Staff*	Pay well for high performance and fire any poor performers.	Build a quality team of well paid, loyal and motivated employees.	Employ members of family and friends wherever possible.

Table 3.5 (Cont'd)

POSSIBLE CONSEQUENCES OF THE CORPORATE OBJECTIVES			
(a) *Business*	Eventually a conglomerate business. Growth by acquisition.	Build company from within not by acquisition. Remain specialized.	Remain small and locally orientated.
(b) *Growth Rate*	Take large risks. Accept a high level of borrowings and equity dilution if personal stockholding becomes valuable more quickly as a result.	A need to take some risks but keep these contained to avoid losing the growth trend. External finance and shareholders acceptable in some circumstances.	Take minimum risks. Not keen on borrowing. Dislike the idea of outside shareholders.
(c) *Staff*	Some staff turnover is acceptable. Loyalty may not be high.	Stable staff group who identify with the company.	Family business with reluctance to have outsiders involved. High loyalty.

The above examples illustrate the close connection between risks and objectives. You will see that example A in Table 3.5 seeks high growth and quick profit but that this involves high risk. On the other hand example C accepts limited growth and involves minimum risk. Thus your earlier thinking on risks and other constraints may well need to influence the personal and corporate objectives you can set.

How to proceed

You should now work systematically through the many items which will affect the final plan referring, where necessary, to Table 3.4. As your planning progresses many preliminary decisions will change. This is partly because the thinking about each will progress and also because many of the individual decisions will be interconnected. For example, a particular level of sales implies a particular staff level, size of premises and amount of finance required. Most important of all is likely to be the need to produce a plan which works within the total finance that can be raised. The asterisks in Table 3.4 give an indication of the number of different decisions which have a direct effect on the cash needs. It may therefore be best to think of the preliminary planning as laying down decision guidelines with some actual decisions to follow at a later stage.

One of the most fundamental decisions is size. It is possible to start some businesses with one man, no money and no premises. However, it may be necessary, or preferred, to start on a larger scale which will involve more risk and more finance. This may produce management problems if you have no previous experience and sales problems if the business is to be profitable within a reasonably short time. You may well find your preferred initial size will be limited by the finance you can raise.

The Market

A business cannot exist if there is no market for its products or services. Small businesses are not always fully aware of the size of their market and what share of that market their sales forecast implies. A small company is seldom a significant presence in the national market for its products but the market which it actually serves may be very much smaller. For example, a dry cleaning shop can usually only serve the inhabitants of its local area; people normally go to the nearest cleaner. It may therefore have a very large share of its local market and nearby competition could be disastrous.

Often the secret of success for a small company operating in a big market is to provide some unique feature of its product or service (such as rapid delivery, personalized service) so that it will have a strong appeal to a proportion of the market. In other words the successful company needs to find a market niche.

This point, and the importance of marketing for the small business, has already been discussed on page 00.

Unfortunately, some companies are started whose products have no market appeal at the price they can be profitably sold. The vital questions for a newly developed product are (a) Does anybody really want it? (b) Can those who do afford it? and (c) How do we find those who do want it and can afford it? It is most important that the product or service of your new company will have a market which is big enough both for it and for competitors now and in the future.

Statistics on the size of broad markets are widely available but a more detailed knowledge is often required. This may involve some basic market research. For example, if your product is new it may be necessary to interview a number of prospective customers to get a feel for market interest. If this becomes an elaborate task you may need to employ one of the professional firms which specialize in this business. Some carefully spent time and money at this stage may save a later failure due to a misjudgment of the market.

Competition

Some small companies do not have any competition that concerns them because of success in finding a niche in the market. However, others need to be concerned about competitors. In any start-up it is advisable to research this at the same time as investigating the market. Returning to the dry cleaning shop mentioned above, a competitor opening a shop only a few doors away could be fatal.

It is usually misleading to think of big companies as serious competition for two reasons. First, they are not going to worry about a small competitor when there are bigger ones with a more important market share to consider. Secondly, if it is going to be successful, a small company should seldom be producing a product directly equivalent to that of a big company.

If serious competition does exist, you will need to consider the means of coping with it. Lower price is usually the first thing that occurs to companies in this position yet it is often suicidal. If a company's products are good and well suited to particular market needs, more effective selling is probably a better course of action. Finally, an existing company which meets serious competition has no choice but to fight or fail. However, if in your planning stages this threat seems strong the question of whether to proceed or not should be carefully reconsidered.

Customers

You should try to avoid starting up without a clear idea of either who the first customers will be or, at least, which target group they will come from. Many businesses fail because sales are not made in the right number and at the right time. Any delay in achieving sales is very expensive because running costs continue without the hoped-for income. This is a common cause of failure. It highlights the need for early sales as well as ample provision in the cash facilities for delays. All possible steps need to be taken to secure orders before trading starts. Sometimes it is possible to persuade one large customer to place an early order which will see the company through its first few months. For example, a new consumer product can sometimes be sold to a large multiple retailer.

The conventional wisdom is that too much dependence on one customer is dangerous. While this is certainly true for an established company, for a start-up the advantages of guaranteed early sales are likely to outweigh the risks. Nevertheless, as time passes on the company will still need gradually to reduce the dependence by finding further customers.

An important aspect of your customers is the amount of credit they may require. Some companies work on fixed credit terms whereas others will be open to a negotiation between price and credit. It is unwise to agree to a low profit margin just to avoid giving credit but an element of price reduction may be necessary to keep the credit period, and hence the finance required, within acceptable limits. However, a customer will almost always look for a price reduction which is higher than the cost of borrowing to cover the longer credit period.

Products

A product or service is only commercially viable if it satisfies a market demand. If your product is new the market demand will need to be tested.

It is important that your new business has enough money to complete the development of its first product. Otherwise it will fail before it ever attempts to sell anything. Ideally, the business should not be started before the product is fully developed. This is not always possible but can, for example, sometimes be done by spare time work before giving up employment.

The reliability of a product is at least as important as designing it for economic manufacture. Many a business has failed because its products were unreliable and servicing or replacement costs proved overburdening. Full testing is the only way of avoiding this problem.

Finally, overdependence on just one product can be dangerous because the product may become out of date or be bettered by the competition.

Patents

Most people who believe they have a unique invention consider patenting it. A patent gives protection from the idea being copied by competitors for a number of years. This can ensure a long period of profit from an invention before others are permitted to make similar products.

The process of obtaining a patent is relatively simple. Patents can be registered provided the required fee is paid and the idea is sufficiently original. Not all ideas are patentable. Patent agents or lawyers can be employed to investigate – but not confirm – originality and make the necessary registrations. These usually relate only to the countries in which the patents are registered and the more countries chosen the higher the fees will be. Having successfully registered a patent in the chosen countries an annual renewal fee will also usually be required. These costs can be considerable.

There are many business ideas which have benefitted from patent registration. These include the Xerox copying process, Polaroid photography and many drugs. However, the main drawback is the cost of litigation if a breach of the patent is suspected. Whilst a major corporation with a real winner on its hands will always fight copying, a small company often cannot do so because of cost. In such a case a patent can be of limited advantage. As a result, many businesses choose not to register patents but prefer to stay ahead of the competition by carefully directed research and development.

A patent can have a particular value to an inventor if he does not wish to exploit the commercial potential himself. With the benefit of such protection, an alternative is to license the manufacture of the product to others in exchange for a royalty on sales. This leaves the inventor free to move on to his next idea.

In summary, a patent is no guarantee of commercial success (many inventors register ideas with limited commercial application) or complete protection against competition. You will need to consider the pros and cons carefully with a good lawyer and agent specializing in the field.

Besides patent registration other aspects of your business can be protected by law. For example, your company trade marks can be registered in a similar manner which prohibits others from using your clever choice of name or logo. Again, the author of original published material (which includes other things besides the written word e.g. films and music), in theory, is protected from unauthorized copying by the copyright laws. As with patents the problem is the legal cost of enforcement.

Production

If your new company will make a product, the most important question to ask at the outset is whether to manufacture yourself or to subcontract. If your products are highly technical and difficult to manufacture, or manufacture involves trade secrets, you may have no choice but to manufacture at least part of the product. In other cases, you may have greater freedom of choice.

Most people are too readily tempted to manufacture for the sake of it. There are a number of problems with this, some of the most important of which are:

1 Manufacturing involves capital investment and thus more money.

2 If the production facility is not fully used the unit cost will be disadvantageously high.

3 Production difficulties can absorb a disproportionate amount of management time.

4 You may not have production skills. If you do not, production becomes an added risk of failure.

5 As sales are very difficult to forecast at first it can be difficult to decide what level of production facilities to install. Too much means costs are too high. Too little means orders cannot be fulfilled.

When subcontracting is used it avoids all of these problems. However, it also may have some drawbacks, the most important of which are:

1 Costs will often be higher than for a fully used own facility because the subcontractor needs his own profit.

2 Quality can be harder to control. A good choice of subcontractor is vital to avoid this problem.

3 Late deliveries can be hard to control. Again the choice of subcontractor is important.

4 If the process is very technical an adequate subcontractor may not be available.

5 If commercial secrets are involved subcontracting may be risky.

On balance, you should seriously consider subcontracting at least in the early stages. None of the drawbacks need be fundamental if care is taken in choice of subcontractor and the advantages can be substantial. You will need to check the subcontractor's motivation and priorities to be sure of how well he will try to help you. On the other hand, if processes are too technical or commercially sensitive it will be necessary to do some manufacturing yourself. However, even then some parts of the manufacture may be suitable for subcontracting.

Once your business is fully running cost arguments may favour a change to own manufacture. The business will then almost certainly be better placed to raise the extra money.

Pricing

Pricing is a complex subject. However, most systems are based on either cost-plus pricing or market based pricing. In the former, the costs of making the product or providing the service are calculated and a mark up is added to calculate the final price. For example, a garage may charge for its services at materials cost plus an hourly rate for labour which might be three times the mechanic's wages. This multiple is intended to cover overheads and profit which it will not unless the garage is doing a certain level of business.

In market-based pricing, prices are charged depending on what the customer (or market) will bear. This must, of course, be a price above the company's total costs or losses will be made. A new product may command a price in the market place which is many times its cost if it is unique, highly desirable or much cheaper to make than the competing equivalent products.

Many companies use variable pricing. At its simplest this is a discount structure for bulk buying. For example, bricks might be priced at a basic selling price of £10 per 100 with a discount of 10% on orders of 1,000, 20% on 10,000 and 30% on 100,000. The reason is that many of the costs of each sale are fixed and so a higher proportion of the difference between basic selling price and cost of purchase can be given to a customer placing a large order. This also encourages large and economic orders.

Further details of pricing are given in some of the books on the reading list. There is no doubt that many small companies do not give the subject sufficient thought and underpricing is more common than the reverse.

Finally, you should recognize that pricing is a different subject to costing. The latter, which is briefly discussed on page 124, is about calculating the costs of making and selling a product and is not necessarily related to the price at which products are sold (or could sell). Obviously, if a business is to be profitable its total income (number of goods sold × prices) must be greater than total costs. This is why a knowledge of costs *and* correct pricing are both so important.

Suppliers

Potential suppliers should be identified during planning and answers to the following questions obtained:

1 *Availability* Will supplies always be available in the quantities required? This may affect the number of suppliers required.
2 *Quality* Is the quality acceptable and reliably so? Some suppliers may be best left alone if the quality of goods is suspect.
3 *Delivery* What guarantee is there of reliable delivery dates? This may affect the minimum stock levels that must be carried for safety.
4 *After Sales Service* If required, is it of an acceptable standard? Your customer relationships may depend on this.
5 *Price* What price is available and what, if any, is the discount situation? This may influence the sensible minimum order size.
6 *Credit* How much credit can be obtained? This will affect cash requirements. Your new business may not be able to get any credit for its first few months.

Obviously not all answers to these questions will be reliable from the supplier himself and you should make enquiries within the trade. It is likely that the answers do not point to one best supplier. For example, if all other aspects are excellent it is unlikely that price will be. A compromise decision may be necessary and the question of credit may dominate to begin with. It is also important to recognize that relationships with suppliers are as important as relationships with customers. This is particularly so if you are planning to sell a limited range of bought-in finished goods, perhaps as an exclusive distributor. Finally, it makes sense not to be committed to just one supplier though in the early days this may be necessary to use bulk buying to get prices down to an acceptable level.

Premises

Premises for a small business can be hard to find. The possibilities may be limited by constraints such as delivery needs, directors' personal circumstances or the ability to recruit staff. Premises which are small enough are also often hard to find.

A common wish is to purchase premises. While there are some good arguments for an established business doing so, there are few circumstances when a start-up should seek a freehold. This is because it increases the amount of finance required. Also, it is likely that in the important early years, interest and repayments on the borrowing will together be more than rent at a time when minimum cash outgoings are wanted.

If your company is to lease premises you need to think about the following factors:

1 What is the minimum size of premises for early needs? You should not be overly concerned with future growth. You first have to survive.
2 What is the rent plus rates per square foot? Nowadays rates are a real burden and vary greatly from area to area so a rent comparison alone is not good enough.
3 Will a start-up business be an acceptable tenant to the landlord? The presence of a substantial investor or a financial institution can be an advantage.
4 How long is the lease and when are rent reviews? Too short a lease could force you to move before you are ready. A long lease will need to be assignable to a new tenant if you wish to move before it terminates.

It must have already become clear that finding suitable premises can be one of the most difficult aspects of starting a business. Who then can help? The main possibilities are:

1 Estate agents. They provide a similar service for commercial as for domestic property.
2 Local authorities. Many of these have industrial officers whose job is to aid local industry. Some local authorities have their own premises for rent and in

certain parts of the country (e.g. Wales, North East) grants and/or rent free periods are available to new businesses.

3 New Town Development Corporations. Their role is similar to local authority departments.

4 Recent legislation has given tax allowances to individuals who invest in small industrial units (known as 'small workshops'). As many of these individuals will have formed consortia for the purpose through firms of chartered accountants, this is a possible means of enquiry.

Finally, it is worth being aware that there are a number of developments around the country where space is more flexible than normal and other services are provided. An example is The Barley Mow, Chiswick, London W4. In this large building tenants can rent from 100 square feet upwards and the size of their space can be increased fairly easily. An inclusive rent is charged which covers heat, light and the use of a telephonist/receptionist. Small companies in the complex can provide typing, photocopying, canteen and other services a very small business would otherwise find expensive. Unfortunately there are not many of these developments. Any of the sources listed above might know of them as would your local office of the Department of Industry's Small Firms Service.

Plant and Equipment

Your new business may need plant and machinery if it is to manufacture a product and will certainly need office fittings, furniture and equipment. This can involve large sums of money, particularly if bare premises are rented which need screens, carpets, heaters and light fittings. Office equipment will include desks, typewriters, telephones and telex. Motor vehicles, including cars, are also included under this heading.

The list of needs will be long and you should prepare it carefully. Depending on finance available serious consideration will need to be given to whether you should hire purchase or lease some or all of this list of items. These two means of finance have important differences which are discussed on page 65.

You should aim to start with as little plant and equipment as possible. In other words, run as lean as possible and defer less essential purchases until your business is cash generating. This is discussed again on pages 60 and 63.

Partners and Staff

It is likely by this stage that your partners in the new enterprise have been identified but you need to be aware of several points. A business relationship in a new company (which may hit difficulties or even fail) will often be under greater stress than an ordinary friendship. It is common for instance, if two people are involved, to have 50/50 shareholdings and be joint managing directors. This is a dangerous recipe as there is no formula to solve basic disagreements. It is better to have a slight split of power or appoint a chairman who has the casting vote if disagreements need to be resolved. If your new business is to run as a partnership, rather than a limited company, a proper formal legal partnership agreement should be drawn up by solicitors partly for this purpose. Many businesses in difficulty have failed because the two partners were fighting each other instead of their problems.

A new company with several founders seems a secure arrangement. One danger, however, is that it is easy for a small group of people to believe they have all the skilled functions covered when it is not true. For example, can anyone really do accounting? Again, an agreed management structure and share split will have to be made at an early stage or problems are inevitable.

Turning to employees seems easy after the minefield surrounding partners but care is still necessary. A number of questions need to be considered:

1 Can enough skilled people be found locally?
2 What are the going wage rates?
3 Will the new company pay (a) the least it can get away with (b) the same rate as everybody else (c) higher rates to attract the very best?
4 What will the policy be towards crisis and possible redundancies?
5 To what extent will employees be involved in running the business? Will they be offered shares?
6 How many are needed at first?
7 What about pensions, sickness, holidays, injuries etc?

This list is not exhaustive but it is already daunting. You will need to learn all the regulations (both central and local government) which the company must satisfy when employing people. Further detail is given on page 112. Help is likely to be needed. At this early stage, though, the important decision will be the company's policy towards its employees. Many of the detailed decisions will then follow more easily.

Finally, and very importantly, you will need to draw up a list of initial employee requirements including type of person, names where known, and likely cost leading to a total salary bill which will be needed for forecasting.

The importance of getting the 'people' side right is emphasized on page 146.

Working Capital

Working capital has a number of definitions but we can simply consider it as the money needed to finance the day-to-day running of the business rather than its essential longer-term purchases such as premises, plant, office equipment. The latter are called 'fixed assets' by accountants and assets which are frequently changing (such as stock) are called 'current assets'. The major components of current assets are stock and debtors, the latter being the amounts of money owed to the business usually by customers. One contribution to financing stock and debtors is creditors, which are the amounts of money owed by the business to its suppliers. Obviously, if sufficient credit could be taken to cover all amounts owed to the business only stock would have to be financed. The amount of credit given, and taken, will depend on two main factors – the industry (i.e. what is common for that trade) and the new company (i.e. how much credit it can get from suppliers).

In the early stages of any new business, wages, rent and supplies must be paid for during the loss-making period when there are no sales. This all requires cash. Even when the business is running on an even keel, working capital (i.e. the finance needed for stock + debtors − creditors) will be required. These two elements – the build up finance while losses are made and the continuing finance – need careful calculation, otherwise insufficient working capital may be available resulting in cash difficulties.

It will now be obvious that the amount of working capital you require is one of the most important aspects of your total cash needs. It is discussed more fully in the next chapter but a preliminary estimate can be made. This estimate is the sum of the running costs until breakeven is reached (which is approximately when income equals outgoings) and the equation, stock plus debtors minus creditors to operate at the required level of turnover. Although only a crude estimate, this will give a first indication of working capital requirements to aid your further planning.

Investors

Assuming outside finance is required you will have to give thought to possible investors. This is the subject of Chapter 6.

Summary

By the end of this phase of your planning most of the major decision areas will have been considered and preliminary thought given to each. The exploration of the consequences of these interlinked elements of the plan through a cash flow and profit forecast are then essential as finance may be a crucial constraint on the ways in which your new business can develop.

It has been stressed that each decision area needs to be thought through systematically if later problems are to be avoided. These can occur in a large number of different areas. The planning process should certainly help you to avoid some of the possible problems and it will also give you a framework against which to take action as problems occur. Careful planning will thus help reduce the risks of failure. However, some risks are an inherent part of business life and it is essential that you consider them very carefully because bankruptcy is a possible consequence of bad misjudgment.

4

Profit and Cash Forecasting

Introduction

In Chapter 3 the preparation of a business plan was discussed. It is now possible to prepare numerical forecasts of cash and profit to validate your planning. The aim of this chapter is to discuss thoroughly how to prepare these forecasts which are essential if you wish to succeed.

Your forecasts will indicate how much finance is needed to trade assuming your plans are achieved. As your new business may easily fail through shortage of finance it is crucial that the forecasts are prepared conservatively. This means that they should err in the direction of caution and not be optimistic estimates. For example, sales should be forecast at a level which it is believed will be comfortably achieved – though this can be hard with a new business. Correspondingly, overheads should be adequately allowed for. Generous allowances for expenses not known in detail are sensible. Finally, because great uncertainties are likely to remain, you should examine the effects of possible errors in the level of sales and other important variables (this is known as a sensitivity analysis). All these points are discussed in this chapter.

In addition to validating your planning, your forecasts can form the basis of a system to monitor early performance of your business by comparing actual results with forecast. The variances (which are the differences between forecast and actual numbers) will be important pointers towards any corrective action that might then be needed to return to your planned path. This is one aspect of the financial control of a business which is discussed further in Chapter 8.

What are Cash Flow, Profit, and a Balance Sheet?

This section gives a brief theoretical background to the sections on forecasting for those who have no knowledge of even simple accounting ideas. Those who have will not need to read it.

34

Profit

The man who pays £5 for a cup final ticket and then sells it for £25 considers he has made £20 profit. However, in business life there are overheads and other costs to deduct from this figure (the gross profit) before net profit can be calculated. In addition, in a continuing business, allowances must be made for the replacement of those assets which are required for the company to trade (e.g. plant, equipment and motor vehicles) and for possible losses from bad debts (e.g. the £25 cheque bouncing). It can be seen then that calculation of profit for a business is not simple.

Unfortunately, there are many differing views about the details of profit calculation which are beyond the scope of this book. You should be aware, however, that there is seldom an absolute answer on which all will agree.

One difficult area is the allowance made for the replacement of assets which are required for the company to trade. This is called depreciation and many of the arguments over the level of profit centre around it. For example, a computer might cost £5,000 and last five years before needing replacement. One view of depreciation is to charge £1,000 per year against profit for five years to allow for its use.

Table 4.1 shows an example of the effect on profit of differing depreciation rates for a growing business with a high level of depreciating assets (e.g. a T.V. rental company). It can be seen that the net profit depends greatly on the depreciation policy in this example. Indeed, the 3 and 5 year write-off policies show opposite profit trends, the former decreasing and the latter increasing. Some businesses, such as a firm of estate agents, have few assets to depreciate and this area is then of much less concern.

Table 4.1: The Effect on Profit of Different Depreciation Rates

	Year 1	Year 2	Year 3
Total asset cost (no depreciation)	£50,000	£100,000	£150,000
Profit before tax and depreciation (A)	£25,000	£37,000	£50,000
Depreciation charge (B)			
3 year write-off	£17,000	£33,000	£50,000
4 year write-off	£12,500	£25,000	£37,500
5 year write-off	£10,000	£20,000	£30,000
Profit before tax (A −B)			
3 year write-off	£8,000	£4,000	£ —
4 year write-off	£12,500	£12,000	£12,500
5 year write-off	£15,000	£17,000	£20,000

Another difficult area is the treatment of research and development costs. If your business involves these as a major item your profit calculations should be based on good professional advice and will not be discussed further here. However, cash forecasts are usually more crucial to a new business and have the advantage of avoiding the controversial areas in profit calculations. Research and development, for example, costs an amount of cash which is not disputable.

Table 4.2 gives a simple example of a profit and loss account. All such accounts start with sales and each will cover a specific trading period (usually one year for audited accounts). The layout does not correspond in detail with a published profit and loss account.

Those costs which directly relate to total sales are deducted first. They are called direct (or variable) costs. They include materials and labour used in manufacturing which must be adjusted for stock used (or made but not sold). This deduction gives gross profit (or contribution). It is the profit on each item sold before deducting overheads which do not directly vary with the level of sales (they are often called fixed costs). Unfortunately, the concept can be misleading, as direct labour is not necessarily paid in this way nor hired or fired to suit varying sales levels.

Finally, overheads including finance charges and depreciation can be deducted. This gives net profit before tax. Tax charges are then calculated. In a limited company a dividend may then be declared provided the profit remaining is sufficient to conduct the future business of the company. This leaves retained profit and will appear as an increase in the reserves figure in the balance sheet.

A more useful layout than Table 4.2 for management control purposes is likely to be similar to Table 8.6 in Chapter 8 which shows the separate contribution that each product in the company's range makes to total profit. The advantage of this is that it will reveal relative profits (or losses) from separate products which will be disguised in a summarized statement.

Finally, a word about tax is necessary. To confuse you further, accounting profit and the profit on which tax is payable are not usually the same. The main differences are related to depreciation. For example, a computer may cost £10,000, of which £2,500 may be deducted from profit in the first year as depreciation. However, the tax allowance which can be claimed in the first year is the whole £10,000 (i.e. 100% depreciation for tax purposes) so taxable profit will be £7,500 lower than accounting profit. In many sets of published accounts an item known as 'deferred tax' appears which is a complicated concept partly used to spread tax allowances over a longer period for accounting purposes. This will not be discussed further but can be studied in any good book on accounting. The accounting treatment does, of course, have no effect on the company's cash position; it will simply claim the £10,000 allowance against its tax bill.

Table 4.2: An Example of a Profit and Loss Account for a Manufacturing Company

			£
Sales for the year ended 31 December 1982			150,000
Cost of Sales			
Purchases		51,000	
Direct wages		47,000	
Stock and work in progress:			
at the start of the period	15,000		
Less: at the end of the period	30,000	(15,000)	83,000
Gross Profit (44.7% of sales)			67,000
Staff Costs			
Directors remuneration	15,000		
Other labour costs	15,000	30,000	
Overheads			
Repairs and renewals	1,500		
Travelling expenses	2,000		
Transport	5,300		
Rent and Rates	2,500		
Insurance	1,000		
Postage	400		
Telephone	750		
Sundry	2,000		
Legal	800		
Audit	1,000	17,250	
Finance Charges			
Bank Charges	2,500		
Loan interest	250	2,750	
Depreciation			
Leasehold property	1,500		
Plant and machinery	1,500		
Motor vehicles	2,700		
Furniture and fixtures	1,000	6,700	
Total Overheads			56,700
Net Profit Before Taxation (6.9% of sales)			10,300
Taxation			3,400
Net Profit After Taxation			6,900
Dividends			500
PROFIT RETAINED			6,400

Cash Flow

Commercial life uses money as a common commodity and most transactions can be converted into monetary terms. A business pays money to its employees, for supplies, rent and other expenses and finally sells its products for money. Because these transactions do not all take place at the same time, the movement of the money (or cash flow) is of great importance. Unfortunately, the prediction of the cash flows is difficult and this is, therefore, the commonest area of weakness in many small companies' financial management. The difficulties are easily illustrated. Often credit is taken from suppliers (i.e. supplies are not paid for on delivery), from staff (who are paid weekly or monthly in arrears), the tax authorities (VAT, PAYE and Corporation Tax are paid in arrears) and the bank (interest is charged in arrears). On the other hand, certain expenses such as rent (which is usually paid in advance) and the cost of credit given to customers (who pay after delivery of the goods) have an opposite effect. Again money is tied up in stock and work in progress which will only be released when goods are sold or work completed. If the business is growing, the level of stock is likely to be increasing as, indeed, is the total working capital required. Finally, changing economic circumstances can make forecasting very difficult, particularly if the company has the uncertainties of a short order book.

For your new business the importance of cash flow forecasting is to make sure the business can operate within the cash available to it. If it cannot, it will fail, which is the reason for trying to master the difficulties of forecasting.

It is important to be aware that cash and profit are different. Table 4.3 lists the main differences.

Balance Sheets

The principle of a balance sheet is that the assets of the business have a total number of claims upon them (by creditors or shareholders) equal in amount to those assets. In other words, the assets and liabilities are in balance. This is easy to understand when you realize that, in theory, the owners could sell all the assets, pay off the liabilities and be left with the difference. For example, if your house (as asset) is worth £30,000 and you have a mortgage (a liability) of £10,000, you could sell the house for £30,000, pay the building society its £10,000 and keep £20,000 (the value of your stake in the house). For a business this does not give an absolute value of the owner's stake because assets are not often recorded at the value you could get for them in a sale at the present time. Indeed, the shares in many businesses are worth much more than the separate value of the assets less liabilities. This is because a buyer is often more interested in the profit potential of the business as a going concern than its asset value if it is broken up.

Table 4.4 is an example of a simple balance sheet. There are many detailed

Table 4.3: The Difference Between Cash Flow and Profit

1 *Cash and Profit Timing Differences*

Cash receipts often do not coincide with the making of a sale. The receipt of cash therefore occurs at a different time to the striking of profit which will occur when the sale is invoiced. Cash payments are similar as they often are made at a different time to the receipt of goods or services.

2 *Cash Items which are not involved in Profit Calculations*

Cash is expended and received on items which are not part of the profit calculation. For example, an increase in stock or debtor levels requires cash yet profit is not affected. Again, cash may be received as a loan from a bank which does not affect profit. Purchase of fixed assets is also a cash, not a profit, item.

3 *Taxes*

Taxes do not normally affect pre-tax profit computations and their payment is not normally made at the same time as the calculation of after tax profits. For example, VAT affects cash flow because the dates of payment of incoming and outgoing flows will be different. Corporation tax is also not normally paid until some months after the end of the year in which profit was made.

4 *Accounting Items not Affecting Cash*

Certain accounting calculations affect profit but have no effect on the cash position. For example, depreciation spreads the cost of an asset over its useful life in calculating profit but the cash cost of the asset can all be incurred when it is acquired. Again, a provision against a possible bad debt will reduce profit but has no effect on cash at the time.

---

differences in the way balance sheets can be presented. However, there are some fixed rules concerning the annual accounts which the Companies Acts require. The particular layout used in Table 4.4 is a common one where assets less liabilities are shown as one half of the balance sheet vertically above the value of the business to the shareholders.

One point to note is that a balance sheet is struck at a particular date. In other words it is a listing of the assets and liabilities of the business which was correct at a particular time and only at that time.

Some brief explanation of the items in the balance sheet is necessary. Starting from the top of the balance sheet example:

1 *Fixed Assets* are permanent assets held for more than one year for the purpose of earning profit. They include the freehold and leasehold property, plant, machinery, fixtures, fittings and motor vehicles which are the essential resources of the business. It is normal to show fixed assets at original cost less depreciation. As discussed in Section 4.2, depreciation is the amount of the fixed asset cost that has been deducted in calculating profit.

The total amount of depreciation of each asset accumulated to date is deducted from the cost of the asset to arrive at its current balance sheet value.

2 *Current Assets* are amounts owed to the business (debtors) and other items which will be converted into cash within twelve months from the balance sheet date. They include stock, debtors and cash. Stock is usually valued at cost or sale value if this is less than cost (i.e. does not include any allowance for profit). Debtors (mostly invoices issued but not yet paid) and prepayments (for example, rent may already have been paid for the coming six months) are often treated together. Provision must be made for any likely bad debts (i.e. invoices which will not be settled for some reason).

3 *Current Liabilities* are amounts owed by the business which are payable within twelve months. They include creditors, current tax and any bank overdraft. The major item is usually creditors. These are amounts owed by the business for services and goods supplied to it. It is sometimes forgotten that an overdraft is a current liability. However, even if a business has had an overdraft for years it is always at call. This means the bank can demand repayment of the whole amount at any time and without specific notice.

4 *Other Liabilities* are any amounts owing to others which are not due within twelve months. They include medium and long-term loans.

5 *Shareholders' Funds* are the amounts subscribed by the owners of the company for share capital plus the profits retained in the business over the years. In a family business directors' loans are often treated as shareholders' funds if they have been used for funding the business.

Finally, it is worth noting that until recently all published accounts were prepared on an 'historic cost' basis. However, in a response to high inflation accountants are now preparing 'current cost' accounts as well as 'historic cost' accounts in many published figures. The essential difference is that assets in the first are recorded at original cost (less depreciation where appropriate) and in the second are recorded at a valuation based on the present cost replacement cost of them.

Assumptions for the Forecasts

The previous section gave a brief introduction to some of the basic accounting you need to understand to prepare forecasts. If you are completely new to the subject of accounting you should seek professional advice on your forecasts. It may be that they contain conceptual mistakes or that certain assumptions you have made are not sufficiently cautious. Caution (or conservatism) needs to be the keynote of your forecasts because so many aspects of the future will be uncertain.

The forecasts need to be your best estimate of the performance of the business during its first critical trading periods. They need to be based on realistic assumptions about, for example, length of credit obtainable and a realistic and careful appraisal of the resources available.

Table 4.4: An Example of a Simple Balance Sheet

				£
FIXED ASSETS (at 31 December 1982)				
(after charging	Leasehold Property			10,000
depreciation to	Plant & Machinery			40,000
date)	Fixtures & Fittings			5,000
	Motor Vehicles			10,000
				65,000
CURRENT ASSETS	Stock & Work in Progress	30,400		
	Debtors & Prepayments	25,000		
			55,400	
Less:				
CURRENT	Creditors & Accruals	20,000		
LIABILITIES	Current Taxation	4,400		
	Bank Overdraft	15,000		
			39,400	
NET CURRENT	(Current assets less current liabilities)			16,000
				81,000
Less:	Long Term Loan			31,000
NET TANGIBLE ASSETS	(Fixed Assets plus net current assets less borrowings)			50,000
Representing				
SHAREHOLDER'S FUNDS	SHARE CAPITAL			£
	Ordinary Shares			20,000
	RETAINED PROFIT			30,000
				50,000

Before starting to prepare numerical forecasts you must decide what assumptions to make. This is a vital first step. The assumptions should be recorded as notes to the forecasts. This allows a reader to see the basis of the forecasts and allows him to judge how realistic they are. Table 4.5 lists some of the areas which will need assumptions.

Period of the Forecasts

A new business may need to forecast for, say, two years. Any greater length is of little value because of the increasingly great uncertainties. This argument can be used to criticise the second year's forecast but it is usually necessary to see what trading will look like in profit and cash terms once the start-up period and costs are over. The second-year forecast is often best seen as an indication of the way the business should perform once established rather than a forecast of actual performance. It will certainly need revision by the end of year one.

It is important to see how the profit and cash positions change at frequent intervals. This is because the cash balance can change dramatically from month to month. The forecast is then also a useful basis for frequent monitoring of actual performance with forecast. You should, therefore, break down each forecast into monthly periods for the first year and, maybe, quarterly for the second year.

Forecasting Profit

A profit forecast is normally the first of the detailed financial forecasts to be prepared. The other forecasts depend on it. A cash forecast is a restatement of the profit forecast in cash terms and a forecast balance sheet is a summary of the asset and liability position at the end of the forecast period.

To forecast profit you will need three separate forecasts: (1) a sales forecast, (2) a production cost/gross margin forecast, (3) an overhead forecast. These will be considered in turn.

The Sales Forecast

In any business sales forecasting is fraught with hazard even when considerable experience of past trading performance and market movements have been acquired. In a new business the process is particularly difficult unless firm advance orders are available. This is why market research extending as far as possible to specific customers is so valuable. It is important to remember to err towards under estimating sales than the reverse. In summary, the first year's sales forecasting must be done with the greatest possible care.

Table 4.6 is a checklist to help your sales forecast.

The Production Costs and Gross Profit Forecast

Next you need to consider the variable costs of each sale. These are the costs which are directly connected with each sale. For example, in a retail shop these costs would be the cost of the stock sold. Wages in the shop would probably not

Table 4.5: Important Areas which Need Assumptions when Forecasting

Fixed assets (premises, plant, office equipment, vehicles)	Are costs known exactly? If not, a conservative estimate based on some exploration of market prices is needed. Assumptions about whether each asset is to be leased or purchased outright are needed.
Sales (See Table 4.6)	A good sales forecast is crucial as everything else flows from it. The assumptions must be conservative. If there is little information on which to make a proper forecast, forecasting should be done at two or three different levels of possible sales.
Stock	By the time your business is operating, stock should normally be a reasonably constant proportion of annual sales. You should aim to keep stock at the minimum level consistent with not running out of vital supplies. Few businesses should carry more than 3 months' stock. If early estimates show this look at them again carefully.
Debtors (if not a cash business)	How much credit your new business must give its customers depends on normal practice for the industry and individual negotiation. If the norm is, say, settlement at the end of the month following the month of delivery (average 45 days) it is sensible to assume slower settlement. This assumption might be 60 days.
Creditors (where credit for supplies can be obtained)	A new business may have difficulty obtaining credit from its suppliers. Individual negotiations will be necessary, and may mean credit is only available after, say, six months trading. It would be harmful not to pay on time in the early stages so assume invoices are settled a few days early.
Production costs (where appropriate) (See Table 4.7)	You will need assumptions about the cost of materials and the labour required (which may be difficult for a new product). Major errors can be costly as any over-run of costs above forecast will reduce profit levels. Subcontracting manufacture does produce a reasonably certain figure. The effect of inflation should be taken into account.
Pricing	This was discussed in Chapter 3. It is a crucial area as price less production costs (or other direct costs for a non manufacturing company) is gross profit and this must cover overheads before net profit can be made.
Overheads (See Table 4.8)	Have they all been allowed for? Are all realistically known? If not, what assumptions must be made? Inflation should not be forgotten (and a level will have to be assumed).
Inflation	This can affect all cash items and ought to be allowed for. A realistic assumption about its future level must be made.

be directly related to sales unless sales commission is paid. Table 4.7 gives a summarized checklist to help with this forecast.

The deduction of variable costs from sales gives gross profit which is the contribution the sales make towards overheads and net profits. Table 4.2 which shows a simple profit and loss account, illustrates this. (So does Table 8.6 in Chapter 8).

The Overhead Forecast

Lastly, you must forecast overhead costs. These contain a large number of items a summary of which is given in Table 4.8.

Table 4.6: What You Should Consider when Preparing a Sales Forecast

What customers will produce sales and how much?

What is the size of the order book and its delivery requirements?

What is the outlook for the market?

Will general economic conditions change?

What effects will competition have?

How seasonal will sales be?

Will there be any restrictions on production, distribution or other factors?

Are prices realistic?

Are margins realistic?

Is the discount structure (if any) realistic?

Are key people committed to the forecast?

Table 4.7: What You Should Consider when Preparing a Production Costs and Gross Profit Forecast

Is there enough production capacity to meet the sales forecast?

How will raw material costs change during the year?

How will labour costs change during the year?

Can cost increases be passed on as price increases?

How will forecast margins change during the year?

Can raw materials be obtained in great enough quantities?

Can labour be obtained when more is required?

Has stock wastage been allowed for?

How does change in mix of sales of different products affect average margins?

Will productivity change during the year?

Is sales commission to be paid? (If not, all sales costs are indirect and will be included in overheads).

Table 4.8: What You Should Consider when Preparing an Overhead Forecast

The following is a list of most categories of overheads which will be found in many businesses. The effect of cost increases during the year need to be carefully considered.

FACTORY OR WAREHOUSE OVERHEADS (IF APPROPRIATE)	NOTES
Management and supervision costs	These should include National Insurance, pensions and other benefits
Rent and rates	When are increases due?
Maintenance of plant	Include spares
Maintenance of Building	This will depend on the terms of the lease
Heat and light	
Stock wastage	Include obsolescence
Consumables	
Transport costs	
Depreciation of plant and machinery	

DISTRIBUTION AND SELLING	
Salaries	Include National Insurance, pensions and other benefits
Travel costs	
Entertainment costs	
Advertising and promotion	
Bad debts	
Packaging	
Delivery costs	This will be a direct cost if it is, say, postage rather than the fixed costs of a delivery van
Literature costs	
Depreciation of cars	

ADMINISTRATION AND MANAGEMENT	
Salaries	Include National Insurance, pensions and other benefits
Rent and rates	
Insurance	
Entertaining	
Travel	
Postage	
Telephone	
Rent of office equipment	
Cleaning	
Heat and light	
Audit costs	
Other professional fees	
Depreciation of office equipment	

FINANCE	
Overdraft interest	Remember interest rates may change
Loan interest	
Leasing costs	
Hire purchase costs	
Bank charges	

Table 4.9 (Part I): Profit Forecast for the First Year of Trading of XYZ Ltd

MONTHS	1	2	3	4	5	6	7	8	9	10	11	12	TOTAL
SALES (A)	—	—	2,500	5,000	10,000	10,000	10,000	12,500	12,500	12,500	15,000	15,000	105,000
COST OF SALES													
Materials (a)	1,000	1,000	1,600	2,250	3,000	3,000	3,000	3,000	3,000	3,000	4,250	4,250	32,350
Labour (b)	3,000	3,000	3,000	3,000	3,000	3,000	3,000	3,000	3,000	3,000	4,500	4,500	39,000
Stock adjustment (c)	(2,000)	(2,000)	(1,950)	(2,000)	(1,000)	(1,000)	(1,000)	250	250	250	(1,000)	(1,000)	(12,200)
DIRECT COSTS (B = a + b + c)	2,000	2,000	2,650	3,250	5,000	5,000	5,000	6,250	6,250	6,250	7,750	7,750	59,150
GROSS PROFIT (C = A − B)	(2,000)	(2,000)	(150)	1,750	5,000	5,000	5,000	6,250	6,250	6,250	7,250	7,250	45,850
(% of sales)	(—)	(—)	(—)	(35%)	(50%)	(50%)	(50%)	(50%)	(50%)	(50%)	(48%)	(48%)	(44%)
OVERHEAD EXPENSES													
Sales, admin, premises etc (d)	4,000	4,000	4,000	4,000	4,000	4,000	4,000	4,000	4,000	4,000	4,500	4,500	49,000
Depreciation (e)	500	500	500	500	500	500	500	500	500	500	650	650	6,300
Finance costs (f)	400	400	400	400	400	400	400	400	400	400	500	500	5,000
Company formation costs	3,000	—	—	—	—	—	—	—	—	—	—	—	3,000
TOTAL (D = d + e + f)	7,900	4,900	4,900	4,900	4,900	4,900	4,900	4,900	4,900	4,900	5,650	5,650	63,300
PROFIT BEFORE TAX (C − D)	(9,900)	(6,900)	(5,050)	(3,150)	100	100	100	1,350	1,350	1,350	1,600	1,600	(17,450)
(% sales)	(—)	(—)	(—)	(—)	(1)	(1)	(1)	(11)	(11)	(11)	(11)	(11)	(—)

An Example

Finally, the separate elements of the forecast can be combined to give a complete profit forecast. An example is given in Table 4.9 which is extended

Table 4.9 (Part II): Assumptions for the Profit Forecast of XYZ Ltd for Year One

1   Several small orders have been received totalling £50,000 all of which must be delivered within 9 months. The sales team is expected to generate a further £100,000 of orders by the end of the year.

2   It is not expected that any deliveries will be made until month 3 because the production capacity will not be complete until then. A slow build up of manufacturing ability is expected. The total turnover for the year is likely to be restricted to £105,000 by the need for care in not delivering faulty goods.

3   Selling prices are double stock cost with stock being costed at 50% material, 50% labour.

4   The direct labour force increases from 4 to 6 men in month 11. This costs a total of £1,500 extra per month including PAYE, National Insurance etc.

5   Extra equipment is also purchased in month 11 for £5,000 and one extra office employee is taken on at a cost of £500 per month.

6   The original capital equipment costing £19,500 is depreciated at £500 per month which will write it off in just over 3 years. Similarly the equipment bought in month 11 will be depreciated at £150 per month.

7   Finance costs are a first estimate based on an average interest rate of 15% on a first guess of the average amount of money borrowed being £32,000 (see Table 12). Interest is charged equally each month. Monthly finance costs of £400 are increased to £500 when the extra equipment is purchased.

8   No price rises, wage rises or other cost increases are expected during the year.

9   Company formation and money raising costs including legal expenses are estimated at £3,000.

Additional Explanatory Notes for the Profit Forecast of ZYZ Ltd for Year One

1   All numbers are rounded to the nearest £50.

2   Throughout the year stock has been valued on a consistent basis with 50% of cost being materials, 50% being labour. Other labour is still treated as a direct cost because it will be used to manufacture once full efficiency is reached. In the meantime it will mostly be involved in helping build the production capabilities. Selling price is double stock cost.

3   The stock adjustment is opening stock less closing stock.

4   Taking month 4, £2,250 of materials are used to produce £4,500 of stock at cost. (Labour is not fully used to manufacture stock until month 5). Sales are £5,000 which is £2,500 of stock at cost, leaving £2,000 of stock produced unsold. The stock adjustment is (£2,000) because stock has increased by this amount.

5   As expected from note 1 above gross profit is 50% when labour is fully utilized (months 5–10).

6   The positive stock adjustment in months 8–10 means that goods from stock are being sold as well as all the month's manufactured output.

over two years to illustrate some of the principles. The notes to this forecast are vital as they list the assumptions which have been made. The example is a relatively simple first attempt which may then need refining to include, for example, expected price increases. There will need to be a number of detailed schedules prepared as a background to this summarized picture which are not shown. In addition to the notes on the Table, the following explanations may be helpful when studying the example:

1 The stock adjustment (opening stock less closing stock) should be noted. When this is positive, stock is being sold. When it is negative, more stock is being manufactured than is sold in the period. In the first year, a stock of £12,200 is forecast to be manufactured and not sold.

2 While materials used varies directly with stock made, labour does not. To begin with the labour cost is high because of non-productive jobs and other start-up problems. Labour costs only increase when men are taken on (month 11).

3 The company expects to make a good gross profit (around 50%) once operating properly so, if overheads are kept low, a good net profit can be made.

Table 4.9 (Part III): Profit Forecast for the Second Year of Trading for XYZ Ltd

QUARTERS	1	2	3	4	TOTAL
SALES (A)	49,500	49,500	59,400	59,400	217,800
COST OF SALES					
Materials (a)	14,850	14,850	14,850	14,850	59,400
Labour (b)	14,850	14,850	14,850	14,850	59,400
Stock adjustment (c)	(4,950)	(4,950)	—	—	(9,900)
DIRECT COSTS (B = a + b + c)	24,750	24,750	29,700	29,700	108,900
GROSS PROFIT (C = A − B)	24,750	24,750	29,700	29,700	108,900
(% of sales)	(50%)	(50%)	(50%)	(50%)	(50%)
OVERHEAD EXPENSES					
Sales, admin, premises etc (d)	14,200	14,200	16,200	16,200	60,800
Depreciation (e)	1,950	1,950	1,950	1,950	7,800
Finance costs (f)	1,500	1,500	1,500	1,500	6,000
Contingency (g)	2,000	2,000	2,000	2,000	8,000
TOTAL (D = d + e + f + g)	19,650	19,650	21,650	21,650	82,600
PROFIT BEFORE TAX (C − D)	5,100	5,100	8,050	8,050	26,300
(% of sales)	(10.3%)	(10.3%)	(13.6%)	(13.6%)	(12.1%)

4 Although the first year shows a loss, profits are forecast on a monthly basis from month 5. In the later months the net profit on sales is over 10% which is very healthy.

5 Depreciation has been taken at £500 per month on the original £19,500 of equipment (see Table 4.12). This will write off the equipment in just over 3 years. The equipment purchased in month 11 is to be written off in less than two years.

6 Finance costs are a very rough first guess and may need amending once the cash flow is complete.

7 The second year's forecast has been prepared on a quarter by quarter basis to reflect the greater uncertainties as time goes on. Often, it will be appropriate to prepare the whole forecast in this way.

8 If your company is to sell more than one product it may be useful to show separately in the contribution to net profit from each product (see page 132 and Table 8.6 in Chapter 8).

Table 4.9 (Part IV): Assumptions for the Profit Forecast of XYZ Ltd for Year Two

1 Labour will be fully used in producing goods throughout the year and the cost of goods made will remain at materials 50%, labour 50%.

2 Sales prices, materials and labour costs are expected to rise by 10% at the beginning of the year.

3 Sales costs, administration, premises etc are only expected to rise by 5% on the same date because rent is fixed for three years.

4 An overhead contingency of £2,000 per quarter has been allowed because of cost uncertainties.

5 At the beginning of month 6 sales volume is expected to increase by 20% due to a sales drive. No increase in labour force is required immediately but the factory will then be at full capacity (there is no ability to manufacture for stock; all output is being sold). At this time, sales costs are expected to increase by £2,000 per quarter.

6 Depreciation and finance charges will remain the same.

Additional Explanatory Notes for the Profit Forecasts of XYZ Ltd for Year Two

1 Labour per quarter will be £4,500 per month × 3 months × 110% which is £14,850. Materials will be used at the same rate.

2 In the first two quarters, goods produced at cost each quarter are £29,700 (materials £14,850, labour £14,850). Sales of £49,500 need £24,750 of goods at cost leaving a stock increase of £4,950 during the quarter.

3 In the final two quarters, goods produced are again £29,700 which is £59,400 at selling price leaving no stock adjustment.

4 Sales, administration, premises etc per quarter will be £4,500 per month × 3 months × 105% which is £14,175 (rounded to £14,200).

5 Depreciation per quarter will be £650 per month × 3 months which is £1,950.

6 Finance costs remain at £500 per month and £1,500 per quarter as a first estimate.

Forms

Table 4.10 is a suitable blank form layout for profit forecasting. Table 8.6 in Chapter 8 gives a blank form example of how to lay out a profit statement showing the separate contributions from a number of products. This can easily be adapted for forecasting purposes.

Forecasting Cash Flow

A cash flow forecast looks at the effects of the profit forecast on cash. It is merely a restatement of the profit forecast in cash terms, which is why the profit forecast must be done first. All the profit forecast assumptions will still apply but additional assumptions about payment dates and so on will be needed.

A cash flow forecast differs from a profit forecast for two main reasons. First, the timing of cash receipts and payments often will not coincide with the timing shown in the profit forecast. For example, profit is struck when a particular sale is invoiced but cash may not be received for two months. These timing differences are the area for new assumptions to be made and conservatism is once again the key. Secondly, a number of items affect profit but not cash (e.g. depreciation) and cash but not profit (e.g. VAT). Table 4.3 lists these.

At its simplest, then, a cash forecast estimates the amounts of cash to be received and paid out in a particular period and vice versa. The net cash received during the period increases the cash balance carried forward into the next period. In most cases, the cash items will directly relate to items in the profit forecast. For example, January sales may become cash received in March's cash forecast. Frequently the period chosen will be one month because many accounts are charged and paid monthly. The initial forecast will need to extend over at least a year, as discussed on page 00.

The vital information to be obtained from your cash forecast is whether your business can exist throughout the forecast periods within its cash and borrowing facilities. Alternatively the forecast will indicate how big these facilities must be. The end result may be that you must either take steps to reduce cash needs or raise outside finance.

You have already estimated the amount of income and overheads for your profit forecast and now you must estimate the timing of such receipts and payments before preparing your cash forecast. A checklist of necessary timing assumptions is given in Table 4.11. The large number of assumptions needed can make a cash forecast particularly difficult to prepare accurately but its value more than outweighs the work required. The uncertainties involved also mean that the forecast becomes less reliable as it attempts to predict further into the future. It is thus important to note that your cash flow will need periodic revision. For example, you might prepare a revised twelve month forecast every three months (a 'rolling forecast') once you are trading.

Table 4.10: Blank Form for a Profit Forecast

MONTHS	1	2	3	4	5	6	7	8	9	10	11	12	TOTAL
SALES (A)													
COST OF SALES													
Materials (a)													
Labour (b)													
Stock adjustment (c)													
DIRECT COSTS (B = a + b + c)													
GROSS PROFIT (C = **A** − **B**)													
(% of sales)													
OVERHEAD EXPENSES													
Sales, admin, premises etc (d)													
Depreciation (e)													
Finance costs (f)													
TOTAL (D = d + e + f)													
PROFIT BEFORE TAX = (C − D)													
(% Sales)													

Note: DO NOT FORGET TO LIST THE ASSUMPTIONS

Example

Table 4.12 is an example to illustrate the principles involved. It is based on the profit forecast in Table 4.9 and has been prepared by listing each item of income and expenditure in detail at the time it is forecast to occur and summarizing the totals under each heading as shown.

Taking for example the first month, the company is forecasting to receive £45,000 (A) (from loan and equity subscriptions but no sales income) and to pay out £30,900 (B) in total, resulting in a net cash receipt of £14,100 (C). Thus the cash balance of zero (D) at the beginning of the month is forecast to increase to £14,100 (E) by the end of the month. This figure (E) becomes the opening cash balance for the next month (D). The bottom line of the forecast (E) shows the cumulative effect of the increase or decrease in cash balances forecast for each month in turn. It can be directly compared with the total of cash and borrowing resources to see if action is required.

The notes to Table 4.12 include a list of the main assumptions and should be studied. Finally, you should note the following points:

1 Like the profit forecast, the cash flow particularly depends on the accuracy of the sales forecast from which the majority of the income forecast is derived.
2 Certain items such as rates, rent, and wages are usually easier to estimate, but inflationary or other increases must not be overlooked.
3 It is normally prudent not to allow for uncertain income (a disputed debt for instance) but to allow for all possible expenditure. Some over-estimate of the time customers will take to pay and some under-estimate of the time the company will take to pay will give a more prudent picture than the reverse.

Table 4.11: Timing Assumptions Needed for Cash Flow Forecasting

---

What assumptions are needed about debtor payments?

How conservative are these?

Are any large customers likely to agree special terms?

Will exports be slower than others to pay?

What assumptions are needed for creditor payments?

Are the levels of purchases realistic?

Are the timing of payments and discounts consistent?

Are VAT payment dates correct?

Are rent and rates payment dates correct?

Are likely dates of telephone, electricity bills etc known?

Is the timing of bank interest/charges known?

What about leasing, hire purchase and other rentals?

Are dates of capital expenditure realistic?

Are dates of loan receipts realistic?

Table 4.12 (Part I): Cash Flow Forecast for the First Year's Trading of XYZ Ltd

MONTHS	1	2	3	4	5	6	7	8	9	10	11	12	TOTAL
CASH RECEIPTS													
Sales	—	—	—	—	2,500	5,000	10,000	10,000	10,000	12,500	12,500	12,500	75,000
Equity	20,000	—	—	—	—	—	—	—	—	—	—	—	20,000
Loan	25,000	—	—	—	—	—	—	—	—	—	5,000	—	30,000
TOTAL (A)	45,000	—	—	—	2,500	5,000	10,000	10,000	10,000	12,500	17,500	12,500	125,000
CASH PAYMENTS													
Materials	1,000	1,000	1,600	2,250	3,000	—	3,000	3,000	3,000	3,000	3,000	4,250	28,100
Labour	3,000	3,000	3,000	3,000	3,000	3,000	3,000	3,000	3,000	3,000	4,500	4,500	39,000
Overheads	4,400	4,400	4,400	4,400	4,400	4,400	4,400	4,400	4,400	4,400	5,000	5,000	54,000
Capital expenditure	19,500	—	—	—	—	—	—	—	—	—	5,000	—	24,500
Start-up costs	3,000	—	—	—	—	—	—	—	—	—	—	—	3,000
TOTAL (B)	30,900	8,400	9,000	9,650	10,400	7,400	10,400	10,400	10,400	10,400	17,500	13,750	148,600
NET CASH FLOW (C) (= A − B)	14,100	(8,400)	(9,000)	(9,650)	(7,900)	(2,400)	(400)	(400)	(400)	2,100	—	(1,250)	(23,600)
CASH BALANCE (OVERDRAFT) AT START (D)	—	14,100	5,700	(3,300)	(12,950)	(20,850)	(23,250)	(23,650)	(24,050)	(24,450)	(22,350)	(22,350)	—
CASH BALANCE (OVERDRAFT) AT END (E) (= D + C)	14,100	5,700	(3,300)	(12,950)	(20,850)	(23,250)	(23,650)	(24,050)	(24,450)	(22,350)	(22,350)	(23,600)	(23,600)

Table 4.12 (Part II): Assumptions for the Cash Flow Forecast of XYZ Ltd for Year One

---

1 Initial equity of £20,000 is subscribed and an initial term loan of £25,000 is raised at 15% interest.

2 Initial capital expenditure is £19,500 on plant, equipment and office fittings. These will be cash purchases.

3 For ease of comparison with the profit forecast in Table 4.9 VAT has been ignored. It should be treated by including it in receipts and payments and showing net payments or receipts quarterly to the Customs and Excise. XYZ Ltd will be collecting more VAT than it pays once trading properly. It will have to make quarterly payments after the first six months. Before then it will be a net payer of VAT and can claim for repayment.

4 Debtors will be collected in the second month after invoice.

5 Materials are paid in cash until month 6 when one month's credit is assumed.

6 For simplicity overheads are shown as equal monthly cash payments which is unlikely to be the case.

7 An additional long term loan of £5,000 is raised in month 11 to pay for the extra plant and machinery.

Additional Explanatory Notes for the Cash Flow Forecast of XYZ Ltd for Year One

1 All amounts are rounded to the nearest £50.

2 Overheads are overhead expenses from the profit forecast less depreciation.

3 The cash balance (overdraft) at the month end is the opening figure for the next month i.e. E in month 2, £5,700, becomes D in month 3.

4 There is no materials payment in month 6 because of the assumption that one month's credit applies from that date.

---

4 In periods which show a heavy use of bank overdraft facilities, for example, it may be necessary to examine the cash flow more closely on, say, a week-by-week basis particularly if outgoing and incoming payments are especially large.

Having prepared your cash flow you should ask yourself whether it is sufficiently conservative and how sensitive it is to errors in the assumptions. This is discussed on page 61.

The profit and cash forecasts shown in Tables 4.9 and 4.12 might form the basis of an application for finance. The forecasts show a need for a £25,000 loan at first, a later loan of £5,000 and an overdraft facility in the first year of, say, £30,000 in addition to the owner's equity subscription of £20,000. The cash flow shows a real overdraft of £24,450 so £30,000 would allow a sensible contingency.

Blank Form

Table 4.13 is a blank form for use in preparing your own cash flow forecasts.

Table 4.12 (Part III): Cash Flow Forecast for the Second Year's Trading of XYZ Ltd

QUARTERS	1	2	3	4	TOTAL
CASH RECEIPTS					
Sales	46,500	49,500	52,800	59,400	208,200
TOTAL (A)	46,500	49,500	52,800	59,400	208,200
CASH PAYMENTS					
Materials	14,150	14,850	14,850	14,850	58,700
Labour	14,850	14,850	14,850	14,850	59,400
Overheads	17,700	17,700	19,700	19,700	74,800
Capital expenditure	—	—	—	—	—
TOTAL (B)	46,700	47,400	49,400	49,400	192,900
NET CASH FLOW (C) (= A − B)	(200)	2,100	3,400	10,000	15,300
CASH BALANCE (OVERDRAFT)					
AT START (D)	(23,600)	(23,800)	(21,700)	(18,300)	(23,600)
AT END (E) (= D + C)	(23,800)	(21,700)	(18,300)	(8,300)	(8,300)

Assumptions for the Cash Flow Forecast of XYZ Ltd for Year Two

The relevant assumptions from the first year's forecast remain unchanged.

Additional Explanatory Notes for the Cash Flow Forecasts of XYZ Ltd for year Two

1   The first quarter's receipts are from sales in months 11, 12, 13 i.e. £15,000, £15,000 and £16,500 totalling £46,500. The next are from months 14, 15, 16 i.e. £16,500, £16,500 and £16,500 totalling £49,500. The third quarter's receipts are from sales in months 17, 18, 19 i.e. £16,500, £16,500 and £19,800 totalling £52,800 The final quarter's are from months 20, 21, 22 i.e. £19,800, £19,800, £19,800 totalling £59,400.

2   The first quarter's materials are from purchases in months 12, 13, 14 i.e. £4,250, £4,950, £4,950 totalling £14,150.

A useful way of summarizing long-term cash flow forecasts can be prepared using Table 4.14 as a blank form. This summarizes the sources of income and the outgoings for a period of one year at a time. It is often called a sources and applications of funds forecast (or statement if used to summarize the past year).

Forecasting Balance Sheets

When your profit and cash forecasts have been completed a forecast balance sheet for, say, the end of years one and two is not difficult to prepare. Tables 4.15 and 4.16 give examples based on the previous profit and cash examples. While these forecasts are not as important as the other two, they can serve to

Table 4.13: Cash Flow Forecast for 12 Months Ending ....

PERIOD	1 £	2 £	3 £	4 £	5 £	6 £	7 £	8 £	9 £	10 £	11 £	12 £	TOTAL £
CASH RECEIPTS													
Sales: Credit													
Cash													
Other income													
Sale of assets													
Loans receivable													
Other receipts													
VAT (net receipts)													
TOTAL (A)													
CASH PAYMENTS													
Purchases and services: Credit													
Cash													
Labour													
Overheads													
Taxation													
Capital expenditure													
Loan repayment													
Dividends (net)													
Interest													
VAT (net payments)													
TOTAL (B)													
NET CASH FLOW C (= **A** − **B**)													
BANK BALANCE (OVERDRAFT) AT START OF PERIOD (D)													
BANK BALANCE (OVERDRAFT) AT END OF PERIOD E (= D + C)													

Notes

1 Schedules will be needed covering the detail behind summarised headings in the cash flow.
2 VAT should be included in sales receipts and cash payments. The net payments (or receipts) to the Customs and Excise should then be entered quarterly.
3 Taxation includes corporation tax and advanced corporation tax (on dividends). PAYE and NHI will be included in labour costs.
4 Do not forget company formation and money raising costs which can be considerable.

56

check arithmetical accuracy and, to an experienced eye, provide a general check on the overall reasonableness of the forecasting assumptions. It may be easier, however, not to prepare these forecasts in the early days of planning if you do not have accountancy skills.

Table 4.14: A Blank Form for use in Longer Term Cash Flow Projections

	YEAR 1 £'000	YEAR 2 £'000	YEAR 3 £'000
TURNOVER (for information)			
RECEIPTS			
Pre-Tax Profits (from profit forecast)			
Less Profit on Disposal of Assets			
Add back non-cash Items			
Depreciation			
Loss on Disposal of Assets			
Bad Debt Provisions			
Others			
Add			
Proceeds of Disposal of Assets			
TOTAL CASH IN (A)			
PAYMENTS			
Capital Expenditure			
Dividends			
Taxation			
Additional Working Capital Requirements			
Stock Increase			
Increase in Debtors			
Contingency			
Less: Increased Use of Creditor's Funds			
TOTAL CASH OUT (B)			
FUNDING SUMMARY			
Opening Cash Balance/(Overdraft)			
Net Inflow/(Outflow) (= A − B)			
Loans Already Planned			
Additional Capital Injections			
Less: Loan Repayments			
Closing Cash Balance/(Overdraft)			
FACILITIES REQUIRED			

Other Matters

Having discussed the preparation of your first set of forecasts, there are a number of additional concepts which you will find useful.

Breakeven

Breakeven means no profit but no loss. This is the level of sales at which the business is starting to show signs of success. More importantly, breakeven is approximately the level of activity at which the business can survive without continuing to drain its cash resources.

A calculation of breakeven is not difficult and gives a guide to how realistic is

Table 4.15: Forecast Balance Sheet for XYZ Ltd at the end of the First Year's Trading (see also Tables 4.9 and 4.12)

FIXED ASSETS			24,500	(from Table 4.12)
Less: Depreciation			6,300	(from Table 4.9)
			18,200	
CURRENT ASSETS				
Stock	12,200			(from Table 4.9. There is no opening stock so the final stock figure is the total stock adjustment figure)
Debtors	30,000	42,200		(months 11, 12 sales from Table 4.9)
LESS: CURRENT LIABILITIES				
Creditors	4,250			(month 12 materials from Table 4.9)
Overdraft	23,600	27,850		(Table 4.12)
			14,350	
			32,550	
Less: Long term loans			30,000	(from Table 4.12)
			£2,550	
SHAREHOLDERS' FUNDS				
Shares			20,000	(from Table 4.12)
Retained profit			(17,450)	(from Table 4.9. There will be no tax payable).
			£2,550	

the first milestone which sales must reach. At its simplest, the calculation is as follows:

1 Calculate the monthly (say) level of overheads which do not vary with sales.
2 At breakeven, sales must produce just enough gross profit to cover these overheads. So calculate the amount per unit of sales which is available to pay overheads (the contribution). For example, in a retail business this might be:

	£	£
Average selling price of goods		10
Less: Average cost of goods	6.5	
Sales Commission	0.5	7
Gross Profit		£3

Thus every £1 of sales generates £0.3 contribution to overheads.

Table 4.16: Forecast Balance Sheet for XYZ Ltd at the end of the Second Year's Trading (See also Tables 4.9 and 4.12)

FIXED ASSETS		24,500	(from Table 4.12 as before)
Less: Depreciation		14,100	(from Table 4.9 total for years 1 and 2)
		10,400	
CURRENT ASSETS			
Stock	22,100		(from Table 4.9 total for years 1 and 2)
Debtors	39,600	61,700	(months 23, 24 sales from Table 4.9)
LESS: CURRENT LIABILITIES			
Creditors	4,950		(month 24 materials from Table 4.9)
Overdraft	8,300		(from Table 4.12)
		13,250	
		48,450	
		58,850	
Less: Long term loans		30,000	(Table 4.12)
		£28,850	
SHAREHOLDERS' FUNDS			
Shares		20,000	(from Table 4.12)
Retained profit from year 1	(17,450)		(from Table 4.9. Tax
year 2	26,300	8,850	again be zero as carried forward losses and capital
		£28,850	allowances on plant are greater than profit)

3 The breakdown level of sales can now be calculated:

Overheads per month – say £6,000
Contribution per £1 of sales   £0.3
Breakeven sales is thus £22,000 per month

The calculation becomes more complicated if the business sells a range of different products at different levels of profit because the proportions of each product sold must first be estimated. Nevertheless, it gives a useful quick guide to how high sales must be before the business starts to make profits. In the above example, annual sales would need to exceed £264,000 which might not be realistic within a reasonable period of time. This might mean either finding a way of reducing overheads or even not starting the business at all.

Overhead lead

One of the problems you must tackle is the extent to which overheads must be incurred before sales are made. If they are built up too quickly this can be very costly. At the extreme, some businesses continue to increase overheads ahead of sales even when sales are established; breakeven becomes a horizon which gets further away not nearer. This is a foolish policy and seldom leads to a successful business.

The best advice is to run your business with the minimum overhead possible at all times. Most of all avoid the big company approach of an expensive reception area, large cars and an ornamental garden. In other words run lean. It would be ideal if sales could be made before any overheads are incurred but it is hard to achieve this. Starting up on a part-time basis in your garage is one solution. At the least you should avoid increasing overheads until absolutely necessary. The drawback of this approach can be that the growth of the business may have to be slower than if overheads lead sales but it is more prudent. Another advantage is that cash crises are less likely to develop when sales do not reach expected levels on time.

Table 5.1 in Chapter 5 is a checklist of ways to keep overheads low.

Phased forecasts

For some businesses, it is possible to forecast in a manner slightly different from the one described above. This approach sets target profits for particular levels of turnover. This is only possible if overheads can be varied. In such a case, it is possible to prepare a 'phased' series of budgets (the version of forecasts designed to be acted upon by management) so that the business stays in profit at turnover levels below best expectation. Success in achieving this aim does, of course, depend on effective management action to change over-heads quickly if sales fall.

Phased forecasts may not be practicable for your business if you have already prepared your plans on the basis of minimum overheads. Indeed, in most businesses overheads are often largely fixed unless drastic action is taken.

Sensitivity

A vital question to ask about any forecast is how sensitive is it to errors in the assumptions? For example, it is important to know what effect, say, a 10% shortfall in forecast sales will have on profit and cash. For a new business, sales and the profit per sale are probably the most difficult areas to forecast. Errors in these figures can have a large effect on cash. For example, if a business plan assumes sales of £250,000 and a 40% gross profit, it would be forecasting £100,000 contribution to overheads and profit. If overheads were forecast at £80,000, profit will then be forecast at £20,000. If sales were to fall by 20% to £200,000, the contribution will drop to £80,000 and the business will now break even. If sales fall by 30% to £175,000, contribution will fall to £70,000 and a loss of £10,000 will be made if overheads are not reduced. In this example a 20% fall in sales produces a 100% fall in profit. This is a measure of the sensitivity of profit to sales level. Cash will be affected similarly which may have grave consequences.

Other crucial assumptions are those concerning the timing of cash payments and receipts and these sensitivities need to be examined. A one month delay in receiving payments in the example above will involve a need for further cash resources of £20,000. This need may be short-term if only one or two months' receipts are late or permanent if all receipts are a month later than forecast.

Contingency

The comments made in the previous paragraphs emphasize the importance of accuracy in your forecasting. They also indicate the size of errors in cash and profit forecast that can result from apparently small errors in other forecasts. One reason to look at breakeven sales levels and sensitivities properly is to decide how much surplus (or contingency) should be allowed in your cash resources. For example, if your cash forecast shows a need for £50,000, an examination of sensitivity and likely errors might suggest it would be wiser to have, say, £75,000 of facilities before starting the business.

Summary

This chapter has attempted to put the business plan discussed in Chapter 3 on a quantitative footing. It has been emphasized that numerical forecasting can be very difficult. Nevertheless, a well-prepared forecast will concentrate your thinking so that you can see, for example, what level of sales will be necessary to break even and what amount of cash you will need to continue in business. Once your business is running these forecasts will need frequent revision and comparison of actual performance with that forecast will be important if you wish to remain in control. This is the subject of Chapter 8.

5

Financial Needs

Introduction

Now that your business plan is prepared and the basic forecasts made, it is possible to decide about your need for finance. Your planning may not yet be complete because, as was noted in Chapter 3, many decisions affect financial needs and finance is often the scarcest of all resources.

This chapter considers financial needs and, in particular, ways in which they may be minimized. It is also important to appreciate that there are different types of financial needs. For example, for how long do you require finance? This too is discussed here. By the end of this stage of your planning you should have a detailed business plan including a detailed view of the finance you need and how much of this will have to be raised from outsiders.

Minimizing Your Need for Finance

Table 5.1 is a checklist of some of the many ways in which the financial needs of your business can be reduced. Table 8.10 in Chapter 8, which is a checklist to review the cash needs of an existing business, is also worth referring to.

Fixed Assets

Your new business may require plant and machinery if it is to manufacture a product and will, whatever its business, need office fittings, furniture and equipment. This can involve large sums of money particularly if bare premises are rented which need screens, carpets, heaters and light fittings. Office equipment will include desks, typewriters, telephones and telex. Motor vehicles including cars may also be needed.

The list of needs is likely to be long. It should be carefully reviewed until it only includes the items you must have to run the business properly. The concept of overhead lead, discussed on page 60 is important here. It is probably better to start with too little overhead rather than too much for this reason. For example, office equipment can often be minimal; photocopying equipment is not justified until it would show a cost advantage over using a specialist service bureau. Again, if you are to manufacture a product, one argument for subcontracting is the saving on the initial fixed asset requirement. All these areas need careful review if cash minimization is wanted. There may, of course, be some drawbacks. For example, having to go outside for photocopying services

Table 5.1: Ways of Reducing Financial Needs (See also Table 8.10 in Chapter 8)

FIXED ASSETS	
Premises	Renting rather than buying involves less capital outlay and greater flexibility.
Plant, machinery, office equipment, cars	Leasing or hire purchase may be better ways of financing than outright cash purchase. Some items can be rented which may save initial cash but may be expensive in the longer run. Second hand equipment is worth considering.
CURRENT ASSETS	
Stock	How much stock is essential? Can stock be drawn from good suppliers as needed rather than hold it yourself and pay for it?
Debtors	Can some or all sales be made for cash? Can advance payments be negotiated? Can debts be collected quickly to reduce cash tied up in debtors? Should discounts be given to shorten debtors? (this can be expensive in profit terms).
CURRENT LIABILITIES	
Creditors	How much credit can be obtained? Can credit taken be longer than credit given? This effectively means that creditors finance working capital needs.
OTHER ASPECTS	
Production	Would subcontracting reduce cash requirements? It will also reduce fixed costs and can thereby reduce risks.
Selling	Can salesmen or agents be largely paid on commission? This will reduce overheads and cash needs prior to sales building up. Can cash in advance be negotiated on the signing of orders?
Marketing/ Advertising	How much cash spending is necessary before sales are generated? Are there cheaper ways than advertising? Magazine and newspaper articles can be useful free advertising.
Overheads	What overheads can be avoided before sales are made and income starts coming in?

is an inconvenience and subcontracted production is not so easily controllable. These drawbacks need to be borne in mind as the decisions are made.

If money is tight you do not have to own all your fixed assets though, if money is not a scarce resource, it may prove cheaper to buy. Instead of buying outright some assets can be rented, leased or hire purchased.

There are strong arguments for renting property. First, unnecessary finance is not tied up in bricks and mortar. Secondly, greater flexibility can be obtained by short-term lets of premises which are likely to be too small in two or three years time. Renting of other assets may be economic if they are only needed for short periods at a time.

Leasing and hire purchase are both means of financing fixed assets but they have important differences.

A finance lease leaves the legal ownership of the asset with the finance company which charges a rent to cover both the cost of the equipment and to provide the required return on its finance. At the end of the 'primary period' the finance company has recovered the cost and seen a return and the rent usually drops to a nominal figure during the 'secondary period'. The latter period exists because it is essential that ownership of the equipment stays with the leasing company which will claim the tax allowances (see Tables 7.5 and 7.6). This means it can offset the whole cost against its profits which will be reflected in the leasing rate it charges.

In a hire purchase contract the legal ownership immediately passes to the purchaser who can claim the tax allowances. The contract usually rents the equipment to the purchaser for the financing period but he has then an option to buy the equipment at a nominal price. It is common to have to pay an initial deposit of 10–30% of the equipment cost when hire purchased in contrast to leasing which does not usually involve a deposit.

An example of the difference in interest rate cost of hire purchase and leasing might be 17% and 10%. The lower rate for leasing reflects the effective extra income to the finance company from claiming the capital allowances. There can be strong advantages in leasing if your new company might not make sufficient profit in its first year to use the tax allowances it could otherwise claim. In any case, as tax is only payable after the end of the first trading year, the lower cost of leasing at the time of the payments may be preferred.

One word of caution is that many lease purchase (or similar name) schemes exist and some are not a finance lease as described above. These are often expensive and the cost of each needs to be compared in terms of (a) the effective interest rate on the money (b) the total cost per month which will depend on the length of the arrangement.

Current Assets

You may find cash saving on debtors difficult as the terms of trade of the industry may dictate the length of credit you have to offer. Nevertheless, there is no excuse for not planning to collect debtors promptly. Stock is an area where planning can be very valuable as too much is more often held than too little. One of the difficulties can be the wide range of stock items which many businesses need. The secret of minimizing stock levels is good stock control about which some comments are made in Chapter 8.

Creditors may be an area where you have little scope for savings by increasing credit taken. Indeed, your new business may have to pay cash for a while before credit will be given by suppliers. This is one reason for dealing with relatively few suppliers to establish a level of business at which credit (and maybe discounts) will be given as soon as possible. If cash is tight, you may have to choose a supplier which offers credit but is expensive rather than one who does not but is cheaper.

Overheads

Finally, all overhead areas need a close look. For example, some costs can be linked to income which reduces overheads. A high percentage of sales commission rather than salary to salesmen is one way of doing this. Other areas involving the build up of cost before income also need thought. For example the initial number of staff. Some services can be purchased on a part-time basis to start with if the work does not justify a full time salary. Bookkeeping is a possible example. Your review of proposed costs should ask the key questions, do we need it yet and can we do it cheaper?

Having discussed reduction of costs a word of caution is necessary. Chapter 4 emphasized the inherent uncertainties in forecasting leading to a need for prudence in estimating financial requirements. You would therefore be most unwise to try and cut down on a sensible contingency whose size will depend on a careful examination of some of the areas for error.

The Financial Structure of Your Business

By now you should have a firm idea of the total amount of finance which will be needed for your business. This will include a sensible allowance for contingencies. You can now consider in what general forms that finance should be provided.

A basic concept of financing the needs of any business – new or long established – is known as 'matching'. The principle is to keep the life of assets and their relevant financing of similar length. For example if a computer is to have a productive life of, say, five years it is appropriate to finance it over a similar period. Finance over only, say, one year would probably mean that more cash than that saved by the use of the computer must be found to repay the finance. Conversely, if the finance were to be repayable over a ten year period, some of the finance would still be owing long after the computer was useless.

While matching is a sensible aim, slavish adherence will not be possible and is probably of little value.

You should break down the financial needs of your new business into fixed assets (some of differing lives), working capital and contingency to help with the matching. The matching principle suggests providing for the variable working capital from short-term but renewable sources of cash such as a bank overdraft (this is the most flexible form of short-term capital). Plant, office equipment, vehicles and the like are medium-term investments (say four to seven years of life) and would be suitable for hire purchase, leasing or medium-term loans. Longer-term investments such as buildings, long lasting plant and some element of 'hard core' working capital (such as a base level of stock and debtors) should be financed with long-term loans or share capital.

Table 5.2 gives a summary of the main categories of capital, their uses and their possible sources. It includes some uses such as financing acquisitions which will not be appropriate when your business is very new but which are included for completeness.

Table 5.2: Matching Finance to its Uses

Type of finance	Sources (See Table 5.3)	Uses		Matching Assets
Short-term (Up to 3 yrs)	Bank overdraft Letters of Credit	1 2	Working capital Financing seasonal fluctuations	Stock, debtors
	Credit factoring	3	Financing export orders	Order documentation
	Creditors	4	Bridging finance	Assets to be sold
		5	Minor fixed assets	Fixed assets
Medium-term (3–7 yrs)	Medium term loans	1	Financing fixed assets	Vehicles, plant, equipment
	Hire purchase Leasing	2	Working capital	Stock, debtors
Long-term (7–20 yrs)	Long term loans Redeemable Preference Shares	1 2	Financing assets with long life Long term working capital needs	Premises, plant and machines Hard-core stock, debtors
Permanent	Share Capital Retained Profits	1 2 3 4	Permanent working capital Broaden borrowing base Major fixed assets Financing acquisitions	Permanent stock, debtors Premises Shares of acquired company

Types of Finance

Table 5.3 is a list of the commonest types of outside finance which may be available to you. It also gives a brief summary of the main advantages and disadvantages of each type of finance. The most common forms are discussed briefly in the next sections but reference to the reading list may be needed if you want detailed information.

Short-Term Finance

The simplest and most common form of short-term finance is an overdraft facility. It allows a business to draw cheques until the current account is overdrawn up to an allowed limit. All credit items, such as incoming cheques, will be automatically offset and hence only the amount of finance which is needed from time to time is drawn and charged for by the bank. This usually means it is the cheapest form of finance as well as being extremely flexible. Charges will be a few percent over the bank's base rate on the outstanding daily balance. It must not be forgotten, however, that an overdraft is technically repayable on demand and the bank is likely to object if the current account is not in credit at some time in each month. Most businesses, both small and large, use an element of overdraft financing within their total financing. Common security required by the bank is a debenture (i.e. a legal charge) on all the assets of the business. This will not normally fully satisfy the bank for a new business and personal guarantees may be required.

Credit factoring can be a useful form of finance if your business starts to grow quickly because a higher lending advance against each sales invoice (say 80%) is common than for an overdraft. This higher percentage is possible because the finance house holds the invoice and collects the debt, sending the balance back to the business. If used properly it need not be expensive but often proves to be because it is not used correctly. One problem is that each customer to whom invoices will be issued must be accepted as a good credit risk by the factor. This can involve delays and refusals. Small invoices also make the system uneconomic. It often does not mix well with an overdraft because the bank's main security usually includes the debtors. Nevertheless, when sales are growing fast to relatively few high quality customers, factoring is worth considering seriously.

Medium-Term Finance

The common forms of medium-term finance are a bank medium-term loan, hire purchase, and leasing. Hire purchase and leasing have been rapidly growing areas of finance recently and have already been described on page 65.

A medium-term loan from a bank has greater continuity than an overdraft. It will be for a definite period repayable in agreed, say, monthly instalments over the period. It will cost more than an overdraft by one or two per cent and may involve some restrictions such as a limit on total borrowings of the business. Personal guarantees may again be required if security is thin, which is the case for most new businesses.

Long-Term Financing

Long-term loans are usually less well understood than shorter types of finance and the following features are worth noting:

(a) *Security* will reflect the length and therefore greater risk in lending, compared with shorter-term finance. Loans are usually secured on the assets they finance – freehold and leasehold property and fixed plant and, often, a charge on current assets is looked for. Restrictions on some activities such as further borrowing are common.

(b) *Interest* rates are often fixed in contrast to most short and medium term lending.

(c) *Repayment* over seven to twenty years may be available in a variety of ways such as equal periodic instalments (e.g. quarterly); smaller repayments in the early years and larger ones in the later ones; equal periodic payments of a varying mixture of interest and capital such as the building societies use. Sometimes a 'holiday', i.e. no capital repayments for the first few years, is possible.

(d) *Convertible Loans* These are sometimes used where security is inadequate or where the ability of the business to service the loan is in doubt. The lender usually has the option for a fixed period to subscribe money for shares in the business at a price fixed at the outset or by a formula. If the option is exercised, the subscription money is used to reduce the loan.

(e) *Early Repayment* of fixed rate loans can mean the payment of additional interest to compensate the lender for interest foregone. This gives protection to the lender in event of sharply falling interest rates when his own fixed rate borrowings are not repayable; the borrower is protected against rising interest rates. A variable rate loan usually carries a smaller or no early payment penalty reflecting the fact that the lender is reborrowing his money at periodic intervals.

Another form of long-term finance is preference shares. These are shares in the business which rank ahead of the ordinary shares both for dividends (which are often fixed) and capital. The capital rights give the shareholders the right on liquidation or sale of the business to receive a fixed repayment of their shares ahead of the ordinary shareholders. In other words they have no 'equity' in the proceeds but they are repaid preferentially to the equity shareholders. Also, in contrast to most equity shares, they rarely carry votes except in certain specified situations such as dividends being unpaid for six months or more. Irre-

Table 5.3: Common Type of Finance Available to the Small Business

Description	Advantages	Disadvantages
SHORT TERM *Bank Overdraft (from Clearing Banks)*		
Most common form of borrowing. A borrower is allowed to let his bank current account become overdrawn up to a certain limit.	Usually cheapest finance available; flexible; quickly obtainable; no minimum sum; interest paid on usage only; normally renewable.	Technically repayable on demand; vulnerable to change in Government and banking policy; temptation to use for wrong applications (because of cheapness and convenience); may require personal guarantees.
Short Term Loan (from Clearing Banks and Finance Houses, often owned by Clearing Banks)		
More formal arrangement than overdraft. Lender agrees to advance a sum for a period of time.	Term commitment by lender; often quickly obtainable; can often roll over; improves overdraft flexibility.	Dearer than overdraft (except in special circumstances); uneconomical if funds not really required; may involve some restrictions.
Credit Factoring (from Specialist Finance Houses, often owned by Clearing Banks)		
Finance is provided against each specific invoice. The factor will advance, say, 80% of the value of the invoice. Usually the factor operates the company's sales ledger for a fee and collects the debts as they fall due.	Can save costs if properly used – but often doesn't; credit linked to sales; used properly can be very convenient over a bridging stage; flexible; factors may carry bad debt risk (for extra payment); high percentage advance.	Can be some loss of contact with customers; difficult to terminate; regarded by some financiers as sign of weakness; might reduce overdraft facilities; dearer than it looks at first glance; minimum invoice/account value £100/£1,000 puts it beyond reach of some who need it most.
Invoice Discounting (from Specialist Finance House)		
A form of factoring where each invoice is discounted by the finance house i.e. it lends say, 80% against the security of the invoice. However, the operation of the sales ledger remains with the company.	No loss of contact with customers; can be ended easily; credit linked to sales; flexible; inexpensive and fairly quick to arrange; can be great help in tight liquidity situation.	Might reduce overdraft facilities; dearer than overdraft facilities; regarded by some financiers as a sign of weakness.

Hire Purchase (from Specialist Finance Houses, mostly owned by Clearing Banks)

The company hires the equipment from the finance house for a fixed period and has an option to buy at the end of the period for a nominal sum. Legal ownership (and hence capital allowances) are the company's from the outset. Deposits of 10% to 30% are common.	Quick and inexpensive to arrange; ideal for short life, heavy use assets with guaranteed return, costs and repayment terms fixed for period; does not normally affect bank overdraft; capital allowances available straight away.	Fairly expensive; default may be prosecuted over-vigorously; interest expressed as flat rate can be misleading (a rough rule of thumb is to double the flat rate to get the true rate).

Leasing (usually from same Finance Houses as HP)

In contrast to HP title never passes to the company which leases the equipment until such time as it is worthless or is sold. No deposit is usually paid.	Same advantages as HP except since ownership does not pass, capital allowances are not available to leasee but they are reflected in a lower cost.	Ownership does not pass, therefore no capital allowances.

Medium Term Loans (from Specialist Financial Institutions, Clearing Banks, Merchant Banks, Government and EEC Sources)

Formal arrangement to provide finance (usually secured) for a period from 3–7 years.	Term commitment by lender – costs and repayments known; ideal for financing fixed assets; low minimum sum from some sources; inflation lessens real cost.	Might involve borrowing and other restrictions; dearer than shorter period finance; early repayment may involve additional interest charges.

LONG TERM

Long Term Loans (from Specialist Institutions, Insurance Companies, Government and EEC Sources)

Usually secured. Finance lent for 7–25 years.	Improves financial flexibility; other advantages same as for medium term loans; improves balance sheet; cumulative effect of inflation makes it highly economic in real terms.	Same disadvantages as medium term loans; insurance company loans dearer than they look when linked to life policies; lengthy to arrange (allow four months); may be partly convertible into equity.

Share Capital (from Specialist Institutions, Merchant Banks, Pension Funds)

See page 00.	Improves the platform on which borrowings can be raised. No repayments.	Can be expensive and, if in equity form, will reduce the owner's stake.

71

deemable preference shares usually carry a higher dividend than redeemable (i.e. repayable) shares.

The effective cost of these shares must be considered. As dividends are paid out of profits after tax the comparable interest rate (which is deductible from profit before tax is charged) is approximately double the dividend if the company pays Corporation Tax at around 50%.

Equity

Equity share capital is the most permanent form of capital. The simplest form is ordinary shares. These shares are entitled to the whole of the proceeds of the sale of the business after repayment of all liabilities including loans and preference shares. In other words they increase in value as the business succeeds and becomes more valuable. They usually also carry all the votes which gives control over the management of the business. A simple majority vote (i.e. 50+%) will be sufficient for most matters but a 75+% vote is sometimes needed. Ordinary shares have no guaranteed entitlement to dividends but these can be proposed by directors and voted on by shareholders. In private owner managed businesses dividends are seldom declared because income tax surcharge may be payable on dividends (because it is 'unearned income'); higher salaries (earned income) are thus usually preferred because of the lower tax cost.

If your company raises equity finance from an institution a common problem is that the institution may want dividends but you may not. One solution to this is for the institution to have preferred ordinary shares which entitle it to a guaranteed dividend and do not oblige the ordinary shareholders to receive dividends. The shares are usually equivalent to ordinary shares in all other respects and are therefore full equity shares.

All the above remarks about preference and equity shares do not, of course, apply to a business operating as a sole trader or partnership. In this case share capital is effectively replaced by partners' capital which is not divided into shares in the same way. Matters such as how profit is divided and how votes are cast are usually determined by a partnership agreement and no fixed rules apply. This is discussed further on page 100. There are advantages and drawbacks to each way of structuring a business which are discussed in Chapter 7.

Outside Finance

You should now know your total financial needs which you can compare with the finance available from your own resources. It is worth listing in detail the financial resources available from the partners, relatives and friends before thinking of outside sources as the former are usually cheaper. Table 5.4 gives a

Table 5.4: Possible Ways of Raising Money Yourself

Sources	Uses
Cash savings	share capital
	shareholders loans
Personal borrowings raised by the security of a second mortgage on a house	share capital
	shareholders loans
Personal guarantees (usually also secured by a second mortgage)	security for short term lending such as a bank overdraft
Cash donations from friends, relatives	share capital
	unsecured loans – possibly only for a short or medium term

list of the main possibilities. One useful point to remember is that, as a general rule, the interest on money borrowed personally to buy shares in your business will be allowable for tax relief (similarly the interest on a house mortgage). Unfortunately your own resources, even when supplemented by borrowings, may not be sufficient and finance will then be needed from outside sources.

As a general rule, your own money should be used for permanent capital (shares or indefinite length loans) though personal guarantees of an overdraft are a convenient way of providing for shorter-term needs. As a rule of thumb it should not be difficult to obtain at least as much finance from outside as you have already raised personally and still keep firmly in control of the new business. Considerably greater sums can be obtained if the source of finance is particularly keen on your proposals but, as the outside to personal finance ratio increases, the cost in terms of shares in your business will rise. It is, for example, usually unrealistic to think you can raise ten or twenty times the amount you have available and still retain control of the shares of the business. In rare circumstances this is possible but your proposition would need to be exceptionally attractive to a financier. If, therefore, your plans are indicating this kind of need you may need to alter them to have a realistic chance of raising the finance.

The next chapter discusses the cost of raising outside finance. A word of warning is that it is important to realize that part of that cost is the risk of putting your future to some extent into others' hands. For example, if you raise a bank loan and do not meet the payments of interest or capital on the agreed dates the bank will usually have the power (though it will exercise it reluctantly) to appoint a receiver who will take the business out of your hands and try and recover the bank's finance.

6

Seeking Finance

Introduction

Now that your business planning is complete you can look for outside finance
with the maximum chance of success. The previous chapters have given
guidance on how much finance is required and in what form it should be raised.
They have also discussed the availability of finance from your own resources.
The only questions remaining are (a) Where should the outside finance come
from? (b) How should the application be made? and (c) What will it cost? These
questions are the subject of this chapter.

Sources of Finance

Individuals

Not so long ago it was common for members of a family to provide money to
help the younger generation start or expand a business. This money was almost
always risk finance (i.e. shares or unsecured loans) against which further
finance could be obtained from a bank. It was also often cost free. Unfortunately, the tax burden of recent times has reduced many people's private
wealth so that this kind of finance has been increasingly hard to find.

Despite the decrease in personal wealth in recent years it is still possible to
raise finance from individuals. Increasingly, however, it is necessary to look
further afield than the family. As a result of the recent political interest in small
companies there have been some tax incentives announced to encourage both
the owner manager and outside individual investors. At the time of writing,
these incentives offer income tax relief both against losses and on first making
the investment in certain circumstances. As the rules will doubtless change
with time you will need to consult a tax expert on the up-to-date position.

One consequence of investment by an outsider is that he or she may want
shares in the business, a seat on the board and an effective partnership in the

overall running of the business. Such an offer therefore needs very careful consideration because of its far-reaching implications. Indeed, although money from an individual may appear cost-free because loans are interest-free and any share subscription may be for ordinary shares, it can be a fairly costly transaction. The individual may ask for substantial director's remuneration, an expense account and a car. Finally, an individual is not usually a good source of further finance.

Despite all these cautions, a well chosen individual can be a sensible source of finance, particularly if he or she has professional skills or contacts from which you can benefit.

Clearing Banks

The clearing banks are by far the major provider of finance to businesses. The majority of their finance is short-term and is dominated by the standard over-draft facility. However, banks offer a very wide range of products and are increasingly moving into longer-term lending. Their main facilities are:

(a) Overdraft.
(b) Medium and longer-term loans – the interest rate is normally variable and the majority of such financing is for periods of less than seven years.
(c) Hire Purchase and Leasing – these are usually provided by a subsidiary of the main bank.
(d) Factoring and invoice discounting.
(e) Export Credit Guarantee Department finance – in conjunction with the Government backed ECGD the bank can arrange insurance and finance for export transactions.
(f) Special schemes for small and new businesses.

Government

The Government is a useful source of cheap finance and a wide range of grants and loans are available. Chapter 10, page 154, gives brief details of some of the facilities which may be available. However, the availability of these facilities is constantly changing and the latest literature must always be consulted. This can be obtained from your local Small Firms Information Centre run by the Department of Industry.

Brief details of the main Government agencies are given in Table 6.1. Unfortunately, not all facilities are available to start-up ventures.

Merchant Banks and Insurance Companies

Both these types of organization can, in certain circumstances, be useful sources of finance for the well-established private company but neither is, in general, interested in start-ups.

Table 6.1: A Guide to Development and Venture Capital Facilities

Abstracted from Investors Chronicle (The Financial Times Business Publishing Ltd) 11 February 1983

Note: The columns headed Capital earmarked, Type of client or situation and Rescue Capital have been omitted together with all those organizations in the Investors Chronicle table which did not answer 'Yes' under the heading Start up Capital.

Vehicle for capital	Backers	Min/Max funds injected	Start up capital	Equity stake	Seat on Board	Term of funding	Exit criteria	Special features	Portfolio
Abingworth Tel: (01) 839 6745	Leading UK and European institutions	£100,000–£500,000 and occasionally larger amounts	Possibly if management of proven calibre	Always minority	Usually	Open	Flexible, but happy to take long term view	Extensive overseas contacts, particularly in the US, Europe and the Far East	£25m + in the UK and US
Advent Eurofund Ltd Tel: Jersey (0534) 75151	Monsanto – 50% UK financial institutions universities and colleges —50%	£100,000 to £500,000	Yes but not exclusively	Significant minority	Yes	Flexible	Flexible	'Hands on' management support Significant US contacts. Significant contacts in British universities	Founded July 1982
Anglo-American Venture Fund Ltd Tel: (061) 236 7302	British Technology Group (BTG)	Up to £300,000 but will syndicate	Yes	Yes	Yes	Equity and preference shares	Flexible	'Hands on' management support. US connections	Launched 1981 – five investments
APA Venture Capital Fund Tel: (01) 388 1811	Pension funds, insurance companies and institutions primarily from the UK	£100,000–£1m.	Yes	Minority equity investments	Yes	Approximately 5 years	Generally USM or other market listing	Int'l presence in New York and Paris. High and low-tech Active help to companies	£1.3m in 6 companies
Biotechnology Investments Limited Tel: (01) 280 5000	NM Rothschild and leading UK institutions	Flexible; generally $500,000–$2m; would syndicate larger investments	Yes	Up to 20% exceptionally higher	Normally	Flexible; usually equity	Flexible; flotation preferred but aim to be long-term investors	Active management support. Long experience of venture capital in USA. Team of high-level scientific consultants	$11m in 11 companies
Birmingham Technology Ltd Tel: Birmingham (021) 359 0981	Lloyds Bank PLC; Birmingham City Council; University of Aston in Birmingham	Depending on requirements	Yes	Possibly, but not exclusively	Possibly, but not exclusively	Flexible according to requirements	Flexible	Exclusively hi-tech related enterprise	

Vehicle for capital	Backers	Min/Max funds injected	Start up capital	Equity stake	Seat on Board	Term of funding	Exit criteria	Special features	Portfolio
British Technology Group (BTG) *Tel: (01) 403 6666*	HM Government	As appropriate	Yes	Yes	As appropriate	Finance provided in form of share capital or project finance. Equity, preference and loan capital offered on venture capital terms	Flexible	Availability of technical, patent, management expertise.	About 400 investments and projects with a total book value of £148m.
Brown Shipley Developments *Tel: (01) 606 9833*	Brown, Shipley & Co.	£50,000 minimum equity preference shares, may syndicate larger investments and provide loans	Yes, if individuals have previous experience	Yes, usually 10–30%	Frequently in active non-executive capacity	Equity: open Loans: up to 8 years	Flexible. Aim to capitalise by flotation or sale or require running yield if little prospect of realising capital gain at outset	Other merchant banking facilities available. Aim to establish a close relationship and provide continuing financial support	32 companies
Capital Partners International *Tel: (01) 351 4899*	Private European investors	£10,000–£350,000 Would form syndicate for larger investments	Yes, if management has relevant experience, a detailed business plan and exceptional growth potential	Yes	Yes	Flexible to suit each situation	Flexible to suit company and other shareholders but willing to stay involved long-term	Management support and overseas marketing development	15 companies – £1.6m
Capital Ventures Ltd *Tel: Glos (0242) 584380*	The Colgrave Fund supported by private investors	£25,000–£600,000 ordinary capital Complete package with loan/ preference gearing can be arranged	Yes	Yes, 10–49%	Yes	Equity to be held for a minimum of 5 years	Some kind of marketability to be sought	Managers specialising in finance for new business	New fund
Castle Finance *Tel: Norwich (0603) 22200*	Norwich Union Insurance	Normally £30,000–£500,000	Exceptionally	Yes, up to 30%	No	Medium and long term loans – fixed or variable interest	Looking for dividends: sale of equity when convenient to all shareholders	Supplementary financial services of the Norwich Union Group	Group holdings 54 companies – £11.2m

Vehicle for capital	Backers	Min/Max funds injected	Start up capital	Equity stake	Seat on Board	Term of funding	Exit criteria	Special features	Portfolio
Cayzer, Gartmore Investments Limited Tel: (01) 623 1212	Cayzer Gartmore, subsidiary of British & Commonwealth Shipping	£0.2m-£2m Larger sums syndicated	Exceptionally	Yes. Minority	Normally	Medium	Flexible	Rapid response. Creative support. Other financial services available	6 investments
CIN Industrial Finance Tel: (01) 353 1500	National Coal Board Pension Funds	£500,000-£2m - smaller amounts are referred to our small companies investment fund	Yes, this is also referred to our small companies investment fund	Yes, 10-49%	Yes, when a significant stake is taken in a company; panel of experienced non-executive directors available	Medium and long term loans available only with some form of equity participation	Flexible to suit the company and the shareholders	Individual equity/loan packages formulated to match the needs of company. Support given for acquisitions and developments. Close working relationship with senior management encouraged	£150m in 120 investments
Citicorp Development Capital Tel: (01) 438 1280	Citicorp/ Citibank	£200,000-£5m	Exceptionally; proven management team and high growth prospects required	Yes, 10-40% desired	Often	Open. Structured to suit company requirements	Open, possible flotation preferred	Fast response. Will syndicate larger transactions. Close and extensive overseas contacts through Citibank and US venture capital contacts	£8m in 15 companies in UK. $100m + in over 100 companies in US
Clydesdale Bank Industrial Finance Tel: Glasgow (041) 248 7070	Clydesdale Bank/ Midland Bank	Normally £100,000+ but will consider proposals at lower level	Yes – highly selective	Normally 20-40%	Yes	Open	Running yield with sale when convenient to majority shareholders	Flexibility	6 companies – £900,000
Commercial Bank of the iNear East Tel: (01) 283 4041	Range of shareholders predominantly Greek	Up to £400,000	Yes	No	Not under normal circumstances	Open	Flexible. Good performance would encourage continuing contact	Close working relationships with senior management to promote trust and without unnecessary involvement. No bank charges	Cannot be differentiated from total bank holdings

Vehicle for capital	Backers	Min/Max funds injected	Start up capital	Equity stake	Seat on Board	Term of funding	Exit criteria	Special features	Portfolio
Council for Small Industries in Rural Areas (CoSIRA) Tel: Salisbury (0722) 6255	HM Government plus financial institutions including ICFC under new scheme	£250–£75,000 of maximum ⅓ or ½ of project cost, depending upon location	Loans are available for new starters	No	No	Building loans – 20 yrs. Working capital – 5 yrs. Equipment loans – 5 yrs.	Repayment of loan	Availability of long term building loans. Local representatives throughout the country	2,500 'live' loans – £16m committed
County Bank Tel: (01) 638 6000	National Westminster Bank	£100,000+	Yes for sound projects	If appropriate; often 10–15%; usually less than 25%	Usually ask for the right but rarely exercise it	Loans up to 20 years; equity open	No set criteria – whenever it suits the company and its shareholders	Full range of merchant banking services including advice on financial and other matters; further substantial funds available if company wishes to expand	Over £80m provided in equity linked funding to more than 160 companies
Development Capital Group Tel: (01) 486 5021	Insurance & Pension funds, industrial companies and a major clearing bank	£150,000– £1.5m+	Yes, under certain circumstances	Yes, minority	Yes, in participating non-executive capacity	5 years upwards	As seems appropriate	Directors are all highly experienced ex-industry	30–40 companies – £20m
East of Scotland Industrial Investments Tel: Edinburgh (031) 225 7515	Leading UK institutions	£20,000– £400,000	Occasionally, if proven management	Always minority	Yes	Equity and long term loan capital	Open	Able to formulate financial package to suit client. Supplementary financial advice available. Close working relationship with management	5 companies – £1.1m
East of Scotland Onshore Tel: Edinburgh (031) 225 7515	Leading UK institutions	£30,000–£1m	Occasionally if proven management	Yes, always minority	Yes	Equity and long term capital	Open	Able to formulate financial package to suit client. Extensive contacts in the oil service industry. Supplementary financial advice available	14 companies – £8m

Vehicle for capital	Backers	Min./Max funds injected	Start up capital	Equity stake	Seat on Board	Term of funding	Exit criteria	Special features	Portfolio
Electra Risk Capital *Tel:* *(01) 836 7766*	Private individual investors	£100,000 to £750,000 over a period	Yes	Yes to 50%	Yes	Only equity investment – no dividend	Flexible	Approved investment fund under Business Start Up Scheme. Rapid decisions and close co-operation with entrepreneur	Existing fund to include some 40 investments and expected to issue new fund in early 1983
English & Caledonian PLC *Tel:* *(01) 626 7197* *(01) 283 3531*	Clients of Gartmore Investment, Scottish United Investors and other investors	£200,000– £750,000. Larger sums can be syndicated among existing shareholders	Yes, if management has previous experience in similar markets	Yes 10–49%	Yes	Preferably an equity stake. Loans can be arranged subject to an equity stake	Flexible. Aim to capitalise by flotation	Do not necessarily require dividend on equity stake. Wide industrial experience available to support management	5 companies – £2m. its share-holders have in the last 4 years invested £15m in similar ventures
Equity Capital for Industry *Tel:* *(01) 606 8513*	City Institutions	£200,000–£2m Smaller sums available from associated fund	Exceptionally	Yes, usually 5–25%	Depends on circum-stances	Long term: equity/ convertible/ loan package; tailored to circumstances	Flexible	Long term relationship with under-taking not to deal in shares	27 companies – £29m invested
European Investment Bank (European Community's long term bank) *Tel:* *(01) 222 2933*	1) Scheme operated by DoI and Scottish, Welsh and Northern Ireland Offices 2) Schemes operated by ICFC, Midland Bank 3) Schemes operated by WDA, SDA and Clydesdale Bank 4) Scheme oper-ated by ICFC (under Ortoli facility)	In all cases maximum contribution is 50% of fixed asset cost of project 1) Loans between £15,000 and £4.25m 2) £15,000 and £2m 3) £15,000 and £250,000 4) 15,000– £250,000	Loans can be made for sound projects by new companies with adequate equity	No	No	1) 7 years including 2 year capital repayment moratorium. Fixed rate in region of 10% (end 1982) 2, 3 + 4) Up to 8 years including 2 year capital repayment moratorium. Fixed rate in region of 11% (end–1982)	Not applicable	Priority to small and medium sized companies. EIB disburses in foreign currency but UK Government covers exchange risk for small premium (included in final lending rate)	Over £60m lent since 1978 to about 175 companies

Vehicle for capital	Backers	Min/Max funds injected	Start up capital	Equity stake	Seat on Board	Term of funding	Exit criteria	Special features	Portfolio
First Welsh General Investment Trust Limited *Tel: Cardiff (0222) 396131*	Commercial Bank of Wales PLC	Subject to negotiation	In certain circumstances	Yes and/or option – not essential	Possibly by nominee – not essential	Up to ten years	By negotiation	None	New fund
Fountain Development Capital Fund *Tel: (01) 628 8011*	Hill Samuel, pension funds and insurance companies	£50,000–£750,000	Yes in certain situations	Always minority	Yes	Equity and/or loan	Open	Availability merchant bank services and other specialist management assistance	UK only
Greater London Enterprise Board *Tel: (01) 633 1487*	Greater London Council	Up to £1m but higher in exceptional circumstances	Yes	As necessary	As necessary	–	–	Investment linked to employment creation/ protection in GLC area	–
Gresham Trust *Tel: (01) 606 6474*	Grovewood Securities Ltd (Ultimate holding company Eagle Star Holdings PLC)	£50,000–£500,000 Will syndicate larger amounts	Where experience and track record exists in previous business	Usually, but always a minority holding	Yes	Preference shares or loans: 5–10 Equity: Open	Running yield with sale if and when sought by major shareholders	Gresham director on Board to give advice and support backed by full range of merchant banking services	160 companies £6m
Guidehouse Limited *Tel: (01) 606 6321*	Private	Up to £200,000 directly – syndicate or advise in larger situations	Yes	Preferably yes, but flexible approach e.g. royalty income	If required	Open and flexible	Flexible – tailored to be realistic in relation to the situation	Corporate financial and acquisition and disposal advice	Company and partners investing approx. £1/4m in around 10 companies
Hafren Investment Finance Ltd. *Tel: Treforest (044 385) 2666*	Welsh Development Agency	£10,000–£100,000	Yes	Yes	Yes	Open	Flexible	Advisory service related development capital funds available	Commenced July 1982

Vehicle for capital	Backers	Min./Max funds injected	Start up capital	Equity stake	Seat on Board	Term of funding	Exit criteria	Special features	Portfolio
Hambro International Venture Fund	Various	$250,000–$500,000	Yes	Yes	Usually	Variable	Public offering/sale of co.		5 companies
Hambros Advanced Technology Trust	Hambros Bank	£100,000–£500,000	Yes	Yes	Usually	5 yrs typical	USM criteria/sale of co.		10 companies
Highlands and Islands Development Board *Tel: Inverness (0463) 34171*	HM Government (Scottish Office)	Up to £400,000	Yes	Up to 40%	Exceptionally	5–10 years. 20 years for building loans	Equity by sale	Supplementary advisory and support services. Tie-up with Bank of Scotland and ICFC to form Highland Venture Capital	6,500 businesses assisted
Industrial and Commercial Finance Corporation (ICFC) *Tel: (01) 928 7822*	Finance for Industry (Bank of England and clearing banks)	£5,000–£2m	Yes	Yes, minority	Not under normal circumstances. Nominee director only with mutual agreement	Fixed interest loans medium and long term	Redemption negotiated individually, no requirement to sell shares	18 branch offices, leasing and H.P. advisory services, sale and leaseback facilities management consultancy	3,800 companies – £460m
Innotech Investments Limited *Tel: (01) 834 2492*	Private Individuals	£100,000 to £500,000	Exceptionally	Yes – minority (25–40%)	Yes	Equity: open Loans: 3–6 years	Sale when appropriate Repayment flexible	Management support and advice. Long term relationship Seeks capital gain not running yield	£3m – 6 companies
INTEX Executives (UK) Ltd + E. P. Woods Investments Ltd. *Tel: (01) 831 6925/ 2422263*	Private and institutional investors and trusts	£10,000 to £1m	Yes	Usually minority only. In appropriate circumstances up to 75%	Depends upon circumstances	Equity and loan arranged according to circumstances	Not applicable	Complementary managerial and technical support and advisory services	n/a

Vehicle for capital	Backers	Min/Max funds injected	Start up capital	Equity stake	Seat on Board	Term of funding	Exit criteria	Special features	Portfolio
Larpent Newton & Co Ltd Tel: (01) 831 9991	Advisory work for leading UK institutions	£50,000–£2m	Yes with experienced management	Usually	Yes	Individually tailored	Flexible	Close relationship with manage-ment. General commercial and financial advice	£15m under supervision in 15+ investment
LEDU–The small Business Agency for Northern Ireland Tel: (0232) 691031	Department of Economic Development	£1,500+	Loans, guarantees and grants available	Yes	Not usually	Grants/ loans/ gurantees average 5 years	Repayment of loan or grant as required under terms and conditions of offer	Financial package tailored to requirements. Business technical, marketing and accountancy and design advice	1,000 businesses assisted
Leopold Joseph & Sons Ltd Tel: (01) 588 2323	Leopold Joseph & Sons Ltd and clients	Open	Exceptionally where entrepreneurs have previous experience and can make a sound financial contribution	Yes	Reserve right to appoint non-executive director	Open	Dividend flow, listing on Stock Exchange	Adaptability Full range of financial and advisory services	Cannot be differentiated from total bank holdings
Mathercourt Securities Limited Tel: (01) 831 9001	Private & institutional investors	£25,000–£3.5m syndicated as appropriate	Yes	Yes, 3–30%	Normally. Often represented by experienced nominee	Tailored to suit circum-stances	Flexible, but objective is marketability	Health care financing	Wide coverage; £10m funded in past two years
Melville Street Investments Tel: Edinburgh (031) 226 4071	The British Linen Bank, The Airways Pension Scheme, The Standard Life Assurance Company, Scottish American Investment Company Scottish Northern Investment Trust, The Edinburgh Investment Trust	£50,000–£500,000 May syndicate larger investments	Yes	Minority	Retains the right to appoint a director	Long term capital	Flexible Building up investment portfolio and does not seek to realise investments	Other merchant banking facilities available through the British Linen Bank	28 companies – £28m

Vehicle for capital	Backers	Min/Max funds injected	Start up capital	Equity stake	Seat on Board	Term of funding	Exit criteria	Special features	Portfolio
Merseyside Enterprise Fund Ltd Tel: (051) 227 1366	British Technology Group (BTG)	Up to £100,000 – syndicate larger investments	Yes	Yes	Usually	Open	Flexible. Prepared to offer buy-back	Local fund to invest in companies located in the Merseyside area	Launched 1982 – two investment
Midland Bank Industrial Equity Holdings Group Tel: (01) 638 8861	Midland Bank	£5,000–£2m	Yes	Yes, minority	Usual	Open sale when	Dividend flow: convenient to majority shareholders	Adaptability – £23.5m	109 companies
Minster Trust Tel: (01) 623 1050	Minster Assets	£100,000– £250,000	Exceptionally, where entrepreneurs have previous experience	Yes, minority	Not under normal circumstances	Open	Flexible	Complementary advisory and support services	Not stated
Montague Investment Management Limited Tel: (01) 588 1750	Quoted Investment Trusts	Normally £200,000 to £3m	Only occasionally	Yes, minority	Expects the right to approve non-executive director	Open	Basis for realisation expected but flexible	Flexibility	£20m unlisted US and UK
Moracrest Investments Tel: (01) 628 8409	Midland Bank, Prudential Group and British Gas Pension Fund	£200,000+ May syndicate larger investments	Yes	Yes, minority	Normally	Open	Dividend flow: sale when convenient to majority shareholders	Adaptability	16 companies – £8.7m
National Westminster Bank under the terms of Capital Loan Scheme (Approach through local Branch but if guidance is needed to identify a suitable branch) Tel: (01) 726 1891		£10,000– £100,000	Yes	An option to subscribe for shares is taken by a subsidiary, Growth Options Limited, usually for less than 15% always for less than 50%	Takes the right to appoint a director but rarely, if ever, likely to exercise the right	Up to 10 years	Flexible	Finance is provided in the form of a subordinated loan guaranteed by the directors. The other facilities of the National Westminster Bank Group are available in appropriate cases	73 companies – £3.6m

Vehicle for capital	Backers	Min/Max funds injected	Start up capital	Equity stake	Seat on Board	Term of funding	Exit criteria	Special features	Portfolio
Newmarket Co. (1981) Ltd. (U.K. subsidiary Newmarket (Venture Capital) Ltd.) *Tel:* (01) 638 4551	London listed company with institutional and general public shareholders	Normally US $200,000–$1m but occasionally higher	Yes, but not exclusively	Never a controlling stake	Right to appoint independent director where appropriate	Primary equity; no requirement for immediate income	As appropriate for long term investor	Group has built up substantial experience since 1972, particularly in US and UK; also invests in other countries	34 companies in US – $65m. 5 companies in UK – £2m. 3 companies elsewhere, and approx. $25m in cash
Noble Grossart Investments *Tel: Edinburgh* (031) 226 7011	Noble Grossart and Scottish institutional shareholders	£50,000–£1m	Yes, if the management has good track record in previous business	Yes, usually 20–40%	Yes with active non-executive participation	Open	Flexible but no requirement to sell	Able to contribute financial and general management skills	20 companies –£10m
Northern Venture Capital Syndicate *Tel:* 031-557-3560	Private individuals under the Business Start-Up Scheme	£25,000 to £75,000	Yes	Yes – up to 50%	Yes	Equity capital. Dividends not a priority	Flexible	Approved fund under Business Start-Up Scheme. Funds to be invested by April 1983.	
Oakland Management Holdings Limited *Tel: Hungerford Berks* (04886) 3555	A leading UK institution	£50,000–£250,000	Not normally	Yes	Yes	Flexible up to 7 years	Flexible	Strong management partnership	8 companies
Oakwood Loan Finance Ltd *Tel:* (01) 403 6666	British Technology Group (BTG)	£15,000–£50,000	Yes	10% to 20% by option	No	Option linked, unsecured, 5-year loan. 3-year capital repayment holiday	Flexible	Customer has right to buy out option by a formula linked to profits	35 companies – £1.6m
Prudential Assurance Company Ltd *Tel:* (01) 405 9222	Prudential Group	Typically £50,000–£1m	Occasionally	Yes	Usually	Open	Flexible	Prepared to take longer-term view	46 companies

Vehicle for capital	Backers	Min/Max funds injected	Start up capital	Equity stake	Seat on Board	Term of funding	Exit criteria	Special features	Portfolio
Prutec *Tel:* *(01) 828 2082*	Member of the Prudential Group	Open	Yes	Up to 49%	When appropriate	Open	To suit company and shareholders	Broad technical and financial expertise; flexible in approach and giving long-term financial support	20 investments – £10m. 28 in-house development projects in all areas of high technology
Rainford Venture Capital *Tel: St. Helens (0744) 37227*	Pilkington Prudential, St. Helens Trust and others	£50,000–£350,000	Yes	Yes, but preferably not control	Yes	Primarily equity. Loans where appropriate to agreed term	Equity – according to circumstances. Loan repayment	Backers provide on-going technical/managerial support	7 companies – £1.1m
Safeguard Industrial Investments *Tel:* *(01) 581 4455*	Over 84% of shares held by 17 major insurance companies or pension funds	£50,000–£250,000	Exceptionally	Yes	Not usually	Medium to long	Flexible	Continuing financial advice available	200 + listed and unlisted investments – £16.4m
Scottish Development Agency *Tel: Glasgow (041) 248 2700* **Small Business Division** *Tel: Edinburgh (031) 343 1911*	UK Government	Open	Yes	Where appropriate	If equity taken – right to appoint non-executive director	2–20 years equity open	By agreement with other shareholders	Advisory services, ECSC low interest funds available. Concessionary interest rates in rural areas	£23m in approx. 550 companies
Scottish Offshore Investors *Tel: Glasgow (041) 204 1321*	James Finlay and other financial institutions	£50,000–£250,000	Exceptionally	Yes, between 20–49%	Yes	Medium or long term. Equity or loan/equity package	Flexible – not seeking to realise investments	Other merchant banking facilities in UK and US	6 companies – £1.6m
Second Northern Venture Capital Syndicate *Tel:* *(031) 557-3560*	Private individuals under the Business Start-Up Scheme	£25,000 min.	Yes	Yes – up to 50%	Yes	Equity capital dividends not a priority	Flexible	Approved fund under Business Start-Up Scheme Funds to be invested by April 1984.	—

Vehicle for capital	Backers	Min/Max funds injected	Start up capital	Equity stake	Seat on Board	Term of funding	Exit criteria	Special features	Portfolio
Small Company Innovation Fund (SCIF) *Tel: (01) 403 6666*	British Technology Group (BTG)	£15,000 to £60,000	Yes	Yes, 10% to 35%	No	Equity plus preference shares and unsecured loan	Flexible	Ability to evaluate high technology companies	19 companies – £1m
Smithdown Investments *Tel: (01) 408 1502*	Private individuals	£5,000–£50,000	Yes	Normally	By agreement	Open	Open	Financial management advice etc.	6 companies – £300,000
Stewart Fund Managers *Tel: Edinburgh (031) 226 3271*	Scottish American Investment, Stewart Enterprise Investment	£50,000–£500,000	Exceptionally only	Yes, but always minority and can be part of a package	Not usually	Open	Flexible – but marketability is target	Finance packages of equity, preference and loans available. Experience in unquoted companies	£25m in 50 investments
Thamesdale Investment & Finance Co Ltd *Tel: (01) 629 8322*	American and European investors	£25,000 upwards	Yes in exceptional circumstances	Yes, 10-40%	Non executive	Open	Flexible	Good overseas contacts. Facilitate export and trading situations	All activities in separate holding companies
Thomson Clive Growth Companies Fund Thomson Clive Investments *Tel: (01) 491 4809*	Leading UK institutions	£20,000–£300,000	Exceptionally if management of high quality and operations within specific areas of interest	Yes, usually minority	Usually	Open	Flexible	Management support and extensive contacts particularly in US. Emphasis on technology in portfolio	£6m between the two funds in UK and US
Trust of Property Shares PLC *Tel: (01) 486 4684*	Management support with clearing bankers	£25,000 to £250,000 Syndicate for larger investments with participation	Possibly, if management of proven calibre	Yes, 10-35%	Yes	Open	Flexible Prefer dividends. Sale of equity when convenient to all shareholders	Merchant banking facilities can be introduced	Supplementary group of 6 companies

Vehicle for capital	Backers	Min/Max funds injected	Start up capital	Equity stake	Seat on Board	Term of funding	Exit criteria	Special features	Portfolio
UKP-EA Growth Fund Ltd Tel: (01) 831 9991	United Kingdom Provident Institution and the English Association Group PLC	£50,000–£300,000 but will lead syndicates for larger sums	Only where management has successful track record in related or similar field	Yes, usually up to 30% Never control	Yes	A package tailored to requirements. Loans up to 10 years	Flexible	Continuing advice and merchant banking support if required	New fund
Venture Founders Tel: (0295) 65881	British Investment Trusts	£50,000–£350,000	Yes	Yes, prefer minority position	Yes	Open	Flexible	Seek out start-up and early stage. Strong equity orientation	8 companies – £1.5m
Welsh Development Agency Tel: Treforest (044 385) 2666	UK Government	£2,000–£1m	Yes	Yes	Reserve right. Exercised for larger investments	5–15 years equity open	Sales by agreement with other shareholders	Range of advisory services. Outside businessmen appointed directors	156 companies – £10.5m
Western Enterprise Fund Ltd Tel: (0803) 862271	British Technology Group (BTG) and Dartington & Co Ltd	Up to £100,000 – syndicate larger investments	Yes	Yes. 10% to 49%	Yes	Open	Flexible. To suit shareholders and company	Local fund to invest in companies in Devon and Cornwall. Financial and general advice available	Launched 1982 – three investments
West Midlands Enterprise Board Limited Tel: Birmingham (021) 236-8855	West Midlands County Council and various financial institutions	£100,000–£3m	Yes	Can provide a flexible package of loan/equity capital	Take the right	Normal financial criteria, but prepared to wait for a long-term capital gain	Flexible	–	£2m invested
West Yorkshire Enterprise Board Ltd Tel: Wakefield (0924) 367111	West Yorkshire Metropolitan County Council	£10,000–£500,000	Yes	Possibly	Possibly	Medium/long as required	To suit client	West Yorkshire based companies; joint ventures; most forms of funding available	–

Institutions

Table 6.1 summarizes the main institutions operating in the private company market who are prepared to consider providing start-up finance. The table gives very brief details of the type and amounts of finance which each of these institutions will provide and, through the size of its portfolio, gives a guide to its presence in the market place.

Venture Capital Funds

Table 6.1 also includes the main venture capital funds who will consider providing start-up finance. These are a relatively recent source of finance in the UK. Most are modelled on the American style venture capital firm which has a limited fund of money available and mostly invests within strict criteria such as new technology, specific industrial sectors and a minimum expected return on capital invested. The managers of the fund will often want close involvement in the management of the company. This is the 'hands-on' approach which contrasts with the 'hands-off' approach of many institutions. It would be wrong, however, to think that venture capital funds are the only source of venture capital (i.e. high risk finance invested with a hope of high return) as many institutions are also in this market. Because of the many areas of overlap between these two sources of finance they are summarized together in Table 6.1.

Making an Application

The time has now come to approach a source (or sources) of finance and to raise money. Your business plan should be complete and can, in summarized form, become the basis of an application. It is worth emphasizing that it is important that the plan has the full support of all participants. As first impressions are important, the presentation of a unified front to financiers is an essential part of giving them confidence in your management team and its ability to plan and organize. Remember, too, that you are now in the position of a seller. While you are going to 'buy' money, you will need to sell your idea and yourself to the financier or he will not risk lending you money which you might lose.

Although you will be trying to persuade a financier to have confidence in your plan, you should avoid being overawed by the process. Most of us become irrationally nervous when we approach our bank manager for a loan. Yet if the proposition is sound, the bank should be keen to lend us money which is the way it makes its profits. If you are well prepared and have confidence in a sensible business plan you should have no fears about asking a financier for money. Indeed, if all he does is pour cold water on good ideas you should go elsewhere. The executives of financial organizations are not all of the highest class and many lack imagination. So do not be too upset at a refusal. Remember the stories you have heard of best selling books which were rejected by several publishers before a brave one was found. Even if you do not meet with rejection, approaches to more than one source of finance are sensible so that you can compare terms and conditions. However, this should not be overdone as it can waste a lot of your time and other people's. After a preliminary exploration you should probably concentrate on one or two preferred sources when the detailed investigation stage commences.

It has been mentioned earlier that a professional adviser is a useful critic of your plans and a help in preparing them. When he is in agreement with the plans he can also become an excellent presenter of the case for support to a provider of finance. Indeed, through his contacts he may be able to make introductions to suitable financiers. His previous contacts with the source will enable him to advise you on that source's policy towards its investments.

Time scale

If you are looking for large amounts of risk finance it is important to allow ample time for your application to be processed. Of its nature, a long-term financial need implies careful planning and nobody will be impressed by an urgent request arising from bad planning. The risk involved in most start-up financing means that the financier will quite properly need a few weeks in which to make up his mind. This is not bureaucracy at work but arises from the need to investigate your application properly. Indeed, the investor must go through many of the same thought processes as you have done before reaching, hopefully, the same conclusion.

Presenting your case

If your business planning has been done thoroughly you will be well prepared for a proper presentation of your case. Most organizations who will back start-ups are happy to discuss matters informally at a preliminary meeting but a reasonably full package of information supplied prior to a meeting is always impressive.

If the information is presented in the form of a proposal this need not be lengthy but ideally should include the items listed in Table 6.2. Remember that the impression you give will depend on how well thought out the proposal seems to be and how well you answer questions on it. An example of an application for finance has not been included because the wide range of possibilities would prevent any example being typical enough to be useful. If you base your application on Table 6.2 you will not go far wrong. As financiers are busy men, good layout of your written proposal is advisable. Perhaps the best method is to give a fairly brief summary (say 3/4 pages) with supporting appendices including the forecasts, curriculum vitae, market research, photocopies of orders, product design details etc. The summary should give the financier enough feel of the project to whet his appetite. He can then turn to the appendices when he is interested in studying the detail.

What the Financier Wants

What his assessment is about

Because a financier may lose his money his approach will be very different from that of a car salesman. He will be looking for a return on his money and the actual return of that money eventually. For his assessment of your proposition to be favourable he will want the following:

1 Confidence in the management. There is no doubt that most investors consider the quality of the management of the business to be of the greatest importance. Not only may the investor lose most of his money in a typical start-up if it fails but he may be invested in it for ten or more years, during which all features of the business can change dramatically. It is therefore vital for him to believe that you are capable of adapting to change. 'Are the individuals people who can get things done?' and 'Are they survivors?' are key questions.
2 Confidence in your proposed business. This will depend on market research and a great deal of other investigation.
3 Confidence in the use to which the money will be put. The investor will also wish to be sure the right amount of finance is requested; neither too much nor, even worse, too little.

Table 6.2: What to include in Your Application for Finance

1 Your summarized business plan and in particular:

    (a) nature of business and details of products or services
    (b) market information
    (c) preliminary customers and details of orders (if any)
    (d) profit and cash forecasts together with their main assumptions
    (e) description of the present state of the project (e.g. have premises been found)

2 The names of the key people, how they will organize the management, and details of their relevant experience and skills.

3 The total amount of finance including:

    (a) how you propose to structure it
    (b) details of how much you and your partners can find
    (c) details of any other finance already raised (e.g. a bank overdraft)
    (d) details of what is wanted from the source of finance

4 Confidence in the security. As there may be little actual security available the financier will usually wish to see you with enough of your own money at stake. The financier will be interested as to what your degree of commitment is – which includes how much you stand to lose if the project fails.

In summary, any financier will have to believe in the proposal almost as firmly as you do if he is to risk his money. However, an investing organization with a large portfolio of start-up investments can afford to see some fail provided others succeed. This means it can be more relaxed about the risks than you can. However, even though an institution can afford to see a start-up investment fail, it is not going to invest its money unless it believes there is a reasonable chance of success.

What terms he will offer

All financiers will ask the fundamental question – do the potential returns justify the risk? A clearing bank overdraft gives the bank a profit margin of only a few percent. It will, therefore, not be prepared to risk the loss of a large proportion of that money. This means that a bank will be very interested in the security for its advances. Hire purchase, leasing and factoring companies are in a similar position.

The security usually taken is different for each of the above forms of finance. The clearing bank usually takes a debenture (i.e. security) on all the assets of a new business. Recognizing that these assets may have little value in a liquidation of a new business and that it has little control over the assets, it will also usually look for personal guarantees from the directors to cover any possible loss. In addition, it has the comfort of having its overdraft money repayable at any time. This means it can call in a receiver if it is sufficiently worried about a reduction in the value of its security. In the case of hire purchase the asset is initially only rented to the customer who has paid a percentage of the price as deposit. The hire purchase company then relies on the residual value of the asset to recover its finance in the event of the company failing. Similarly, a leasing company owns the asset anyway and relies on the value of the asset or looks for additional security such as guarantees. Again, a factoring company has the control of, and security over, debtors against which it has only advanced say 80% and has accepted the specific credit risk.

In contrast to these reasonably secured situations, a long-term lender takes considerable risk unless there are good guarantees available from the proprietors. Even if it takes security on the assets it expects to lose some or all of its money if the business fails. This is because it has very limited control of the situation and the assets will inevitably have reduced in value by the time the business collapses. As a result, the financier will normally not be satisfied with interest alone. This will not show a profit for his business after losses have been covered from the investments which fail. Hence a long-term investor usually looks for an equity stake. He then expects to lose all his money in some companies but to make large profits from his equity share in others, making his total investment portfolio profitable.

There are fundamental reasons for raising equity finance which were discussed in Chapter 5. If these are not overriding, your choice may be whether to guarantee all finance personally or to concede an equity stake to a financier who will not seek personal security.

Assuming you are planning to approach a source which provides long-term and equity finance you need to recognize that you will enter into a long term committed relationship. Therefore, you must be prepared to accept that organization's investment philosophy. You should, for example, be concerned with how you will be treated ten years from now. Will the institution want to have a director on your Board? Will it want to influence whether you sell out or not? Will it act reasonably when clauses in your initial agreement need change?

How an investor expects you to behave

Remember that any financier who backs you has shown faith in your plans and abilities when there was no guarantee of success. This should not be forgotten. A financier expects to be kept informed of progress and it is better to err in the direction of too much information rather than too little.

A long-term/equity financier needs to be seen as a financial partner, not just a money shop. He has as much interest in the success of the business as you and will expect you to recognize that fact. He will want to be treated as fairly and openly as any other partner. You will benefit from this when you have problems, need advice and are looking for more money. This fairness of treatment includes paying interest and dividends on the due dates. No organization looks favourably on those customers who are late payers. So pay on time and, if you are going to have to pay late, consult with the financier first rather than explain afterwards when he chases you. The success of such relationships, like any other, is dependent on mutual trust.

Common Weaknesses of Propositions

The most common weakness of applications for finance is inadequate preparation. Once the formal approach is made, any investor will expect you to have thought through your application in detail and will expect you to supply the necessary financial details.

Other common failings are over-optimism and an inadequate allowance for contingencies. It is better to have more finance available than might be required if all goes particularly well. However, it is sensible to have the contingency in the form which does not incur interest charges on money which might not be needed. A bank overdraft automatically provides this and long-term loans can often be advanced only as required.

93

The commonest weakness of small companies is poor financial control. An investor will be very concerned about the future ability of your new company to survive and to adapt to a sometimes rapidly changing world. The plans for control of your business are therefore important. Often the presence of a good accountant (perhaps retained to produce monthly accounts but not employed full time) is a good way to cope initially.

What You Should Expect from a Financier

Just as a financier will expect a certain standard of behaviour from you, so should you expect the same from him. In the early stages, you are likely to be approaching sources of finance with cap in hand. Nevertheless, you should expect a proper hearing from somebody who knows what he is talking about. For example, this can be a problem if you approach a small clearing bank branch with a complicated proposition. Managers in small branches are often not sufficiently experienced to assess such propositions. If, wherever you go, you do not feel you are receiving a fair hearing, then move on. Usually, approaching a new and more enthusiastic source of finance is better than writing letters of complaint as these only cause bad feeling.

Remember that a long-term investment package (loans and equity perhaps) implies a long-term relationship with the financier. It is not easy to unwind arrangements of this type so you should check out the financier just as he will do with you. Before you sign formal agreements, you should feel happy with the style of the investing organization, the quality of its staff and its reputation for fairness and honesty in later dealings.

Normally, your relationship with your bank will be easier to end if you are unhappy at the service you receive. Unfortunately, many people are too reluctant to change banks despite problems. Certainly, you do not want to change banks every twelve months as the relationship can be an important and lasting one. However, if you are unhappy and complaints have not produced the reuslts you want, then change bank. There will be no stigma attached to you; any stigma will be attached to the bank you left.

Summary

Success in raising outside finance can be crucial if your new business is to get off the ground. There is, therefore, no excuse for presenting a poorly thought-out application. Indeed, the rejection of a bad application is probably the best favour an investor could do for you!

There are more sources of start-up finance than many people believe but they all tend to have slightly different preferences and approaches. Some knowledge of what terms a particular source of finance may seek in return for its investment and how it will expect to conduct the continuing relationship with you is useful. Also, as more judgment is required for start-ups than less risky forms of financing, people will sometimes disagree on whether or not to back a particular venture. So, if you believe you have a good idea, have planned properly and are asking for a reasonable amount of money do not be unduly disheartened by one rejection. Try somewhere else instead. Raising finance for a start-up can be a little like finding a publisher for a book from an unknown author – every publisher has turned away a subsequent best seller.

7
Legal and Tax Matters

Introduction

So far we have considered the business planning and money raising needs of your business. Of secondary, but still considerable, importance are a number of legal and tax matters about which you will need to know something. Many of these are formal requirements such as registration for PAYE, VAT and so on. However, one area in which a decision may still be required is whether to trade as a partnership (or sole trader) or as a limited company.

This chapter discusses the most important legal and tax areas which are likely to affect you. However, a word of warning is appropriate. It is not an authoritative guide to matters on which a solicitor or tax specialist should advise with the particular details of your business in front of him. Good professional advice cannot be too strongly recommended because if you make a mistake the consequences may be either expensive (e.g. unnecessarily large tax bills) or disastrous (e.g. becoming personally liable unknowingly).

Partnership or Limited Company?

Sole Trader

This is the simplest form of trading, being one person on his own without partners or a limited company. You will be entitled to all profits after taxation and must bear all the losses.

The main consequence of trading as an individual is that you will be personally responsible for all the liabilities of the business. These may not just be limited to ordinary trading debts but, in theory, could be increased without limit by successful legal action against you. For example, a successful legal claim for compensation due to an accident resulting from use of one of your products could be extremely expensive. It follows that as a sole trader you should be most careful that you can always pay your debts and should be properly insured against possible legal claims. If there is a large amount of risk in the venture you should consider the advantages of trading as a limited company.

Certain aspects of trading by yourself (whether as a sole trader or a one man company) need careful thought. Your health is crucial to the business. Illness or death will stop the trading and you will need to be properly insured against both.

Unfortunately, you will not be covered by National Health Insurance if you are injured while running the business. There are various insurance policies on the market to cover such eventualities. Despite the National Health Insurance position you will still have to pay National Insurance contributions of a flat weekly rate plus a percentage of annual profits. The Department of Health and Social Security can supply details, currently on leaflet NI41.

One advantage of being self-employed is that there is generally a more favourable tax treatment than as an employee paying PAYE. A sole trader pays income tax on all profits of his trade (regardless of drawings) after deduction of all allowable expenses. This is discussed further on page 106.

Partnership

A partnership is defined in law as 'the relation which subsists between persons carrying on a business with a view to profit'. A partnership can be formed for a limited period (to cover a specific project such as a property development) or an unlimited period (which is common when a new business is being formed). As with a sole trader, each partner is liable without limit for all the debts and obligations of the firm. Furthermore, each partner becomes liable as a result of the actions of his partners even if they did not consult him. For this reason a high degree of trust between you and your partners is required.

Normally partners draw up a formal agreement (as discussed on page 100) to cover matters such as division of profits. As with a sole trader, you and your partners need to consider insurance to cover illness, death and legal claims. Partners are treated for tax purposes as individuals liable to income tax on the profits each is entitled to.

Limited Company

It is possible to incorporate a business with limited liability. This means that if the company fails, the shareholders have no liability for its debts except for the amount (if any) not paid on their shares (the issue of partly paid shares is not common).

Nowadays, most groups of individuals wishing to trade tend to register as limited companies rather than partnerships. This applies also to many sole traders who form themselves into one man companies.

The earlier comments about the need to insure against ill health and death will still apply to the directors because they may be crucial to the ability of the company to trade. Taxation is, however, on a very different basis. Generally, the directors pay income tax on their salaries (i.e. their actual drawings) and the company pays corporation tax on its profits (which will be calculated after paying directors' salaries). The tax rates and allowances for income tax and corporation tax are different which can lead to tax advantages in being incorporated or not depending on the circumstances.

Incorporation or Partnership?

There are two separate aspects of deciding whether your business should incorporate or not. These depend on commercial considerations and tax considerations. Some people will have no choice. For example, solicitors and accountants are obliged by law to trade as partnerships and not to limit their liability. On the other hand, the need to raise large amounts of outside finance sometimes forces a decision to incorporate because the investor can then more easily have equity in the business. Otherwise, there is often no simple answer as to which route to choose and professional advice will be needed.

Table 7.1 lists some of the main advantages and disadvantages of a partnership and a limited company to help comparison. There are two main points in the table which need further comment. These are limited liability and tax.

For a new business, the issue of limited versus unlimited liability is not as clear cut as for a mature business. Ironically, a partnership will probably be able to raise less money than a limited company because a lender cannot easily take security on the current assets of the business. Also, the lender cannot easily provide equity finance or he becomes a partner and is liable for all debts which will normally be unacceptable to him. On the other hand, limited liability is often more apparent than real because the owners may have to give personal guarantees to cover the company's borrowings. However, this increase in liability is limited to the amount of the borrowings and does not cover other debts.

As a generalization, a small business is probably better in tax terms to start off as a partnership or sole trader. A mature profitable business may, however, be better off in tax terms by being incorporated. This results from the different taxation methods which are used. It is discussed further on pages 106 and 108. In most cases the final choice should be dictated by the commercial considerations.

Other points in Table 7.1 deserve brief mention. Loss of secrecy as a limited company is often more apparent than real. While audited accounts disclose turnover and profit they do not reveal commercial secrets. Indeed, published accounts may make raising credit easier and there is little to fear from the disclosure requirements. Again, whilst the registration and disclosure requirements of the Companies Acts do require some effort and cost (of audit, for example) these are not unduly burdensome for most businesses. An audit can be of benefit to the company because accounting systems should also be reviewed and criticised.

One final advantage of forming a company which can be considerable is the ability to transfer (by gift or sale) small shareholdings to others without either loss of control or liabilities being incurred by the new shareholders. This is valuable for personal tax planning reasons. It can also ease family succession or the spreading of shares amongst family or friends who take no part in the management. Finally, any partial sale of shares of the mature business to raise

Table 7.1: Partnership Versus Limited Company

A – an advantage D – a disadvantage	PARTNERSHIP	LIMITED COMPANY
Legal entity	D The business has no legal existence separate from the partners	A The company has a separate legal existence.
Liability for debts and legal claims	D Unlimited personal liability	A Limited to the amount unpaid on shares. Directors may incur personal liability in certain circumstances (See Table 7.3).
Death or bankruptcy of partner	D Dissolves the partnership (but can be re-started)	A No effect on the legal existence of the company.
Transfer of shares	D Would normally involve the recipient incurring full legal liabilities and rights.	A Can be transferred to others (e.g. children) without difficulty. Control can remain with the original owners.
Secrecy	A No need to make accounts public.	D Accounts must be filed with the Registrar of Companies annually. Any member of the public may inspect.
Registration etc	A No formal requirements.	D Certain documents must be filed with the Registrar of Companies and certain statutory records must be kept. Must comply with the Companies Acts.
Taxation	Taxed under income tax rules whether profits are drawn out of the business or not.	Directors taxed under income tax rules on their salaries. Company taxed under corporation tax rules on profits after salaries are deducted.
	A Maybe for a new business.	A Maybe for a mature business.
	A Trading losses in the first four years can be offset against other income, including salaries, for the previous three years.	D Trading losses in the first year cannot be offset against previous income.

cash for the shareholders (maybe by flotation) can only be achieved with a limited company.

The Legal Side of a Partnership

A partnership can be formed without legal formalities. In general, every partner incurs unlimited liability for all the debts and obligations of the firm. This is so even if one partner acts without the agreement of his fellow partners. However, despite this general unlimited liability, the partnership agreement can restrict a partner's liability to his share of the partnership capital. This is a limited partnership and must be registered properly at Companies House. Limited partners only have limited liability if they take no part in the running of the business.

Although partnerships do not have to file accounts with the Registrar of Companies, proper accounts must be prepared at least once a year and audited by a professional accountant. The Inland Revenue will, of course, want to see these accounts.

It is not a legal requirement, but most partnerships have a formal partnership agreement. If they do not the provisions of the 1890 Partnership Act concerning profit share and so on will apply. You should, therefore, carefully consider the basis on which your partnership will operate and draw up a proper agreement with the help of a solicitor. Table 7.2 gives a checklist of some of the most important items to include.

If you wish to trade using a business name which is not all the names of the partners, you must state these names on all business documents. You must also give business addresses where they can be contacted. If you want to use a name which would give the impression that your business is connected with the government or a local authority you will need the Secretary of State's approval. There is also a list, held by the Department of Trade, of words you may not use in your name except, again, with permission. Since the 1981 Companies Act came into force it has not been necessary to register your business name.

The Legal Side of Incorporation

Forming a Company

Newly formed companies can be bought off the shelf from a company registration agent. This is quick, simple and relatively cheap. The alternative is to instruct a solicitor to tailor a company to your needs. This takes longer and will cost more but may be preferred.

In either case, the key documents are the Memorandum of Association and the Articles of Association. The first is a kind of charter setting out the activities of the company. The second lays out the rules by which the company is to be managed.

A company can be public or private. The essential difference is that a private company must not offer its shares to the public. For the rest of this chapter only private companies are considered.

A private company must have at least two shareholders. It must also have at least one director and a secretary who cannot be the sole director.

An off-the-shelf company will come complete with a name which can be changed if you wish. Otherwise you will need to choose a name. Names which are the same as existing names will not be allowed. Offensive names or names containing words on a prohibited list issued by the Department of Trade will also not be allowed. As a general rule, names including, for example, bank, insurance, trust, institute, co-operative will not be allowed if this gives a misleading impression about the business. Names suggesting a connection with the crown or the government will only be allowed with specific permission from the Secretary of State.

Table 7.2: Partnership Agreement Checklist

PROFIT SHARING	If there is no other agreement profits and losses will be shared equally. Many partnerships have very different arrangements linked to work done, seniority or capital stake.
DRAWINGS	You may wish to impose limits. Maybe overdrawn accounts should pay interest.
CAPITAL	The amounts may not be equal. Sometimes interest is paid on capital to allow for different sized accounts.
RETIREMENT	Provisions need to be made for resignation, retirement and death. The basis for valuing goodwill and how the retiring partner is to be paid out needs to be agreed.
NEW PARTNERS	Unless agreed otherwise, the consent of all partners is needed. An agreement on how much capital he is expected to contribute is needed.
EXPULSION OF A PARTNER	A mechanism to expel a partner is a sensible precaution.
VOTING RIGHTS	Unless otherwise agreed all partners will have equal voting rights with the majority opinion carrying a vote unless otherwise agreed. No change in the nature of the business of the partnership can be made without all partners consenting.

Table 7.3: A Summary of the Legal Position of Directors

APPOINTMENT

1. By law a private company must have at least one director and a company secretary who cannot be that one director.
2. The directors normally have the power (given by the Articles) to appoint a person to fill a vacancy or as an addition at any time.
3. A director is not necessarily an employee of the company.

REMOVAL OR RESIGNATION

1. A director can normally resign in writing without formal notice.
2. The shareholders can vote a director off (or on) the board by ordinary resolution (more than 50% of the votes).
3. A director is usually disqualified:
   (a) if he becomes bankrupt;
   (b) if he becomes mentally unsound;
   (c) if he is convicted of fraud or of any offence connected with the formation or management of the company.

CONDUCT

The directors must act in 'good faith' and with 'skill and care'.

In summary the rules of conduct of a director are:

1. Utmost good faith towards the company;
2. Honesty in exercising his powers and duties;
*3. No personal profit can be made from the position of director (the company must receive it);
4. The company is liable for contracts he enters into;
*5. If he contracts in his own name, a third party can sue the company as an undisclosed principal;
*6. His powers are limited to those given in the Articles. Other acts within the power of the company need confirmation by the shareholders to avoid personal liability;
*7. He is not liable for wrongdoings of the company unless he is a party to them;
*8. He is a trustee of the company's assets. Any loss arising from unauthorized transactions must be repaid to the company;
*9. If he is non executive and with no particular qualifications, skill and care is a case of doing his best. If he is executive and qualified, the skill and care usually expected from a person of his professional standing is required;
*10. He is at risk if he permits the company to continue trading while it is insolvent, in other words if it cannot pay its debts as they fall due;
*11. He must not fraudulently prefer (i.e. pay) one creditor to another.

* Breach of any of the asterisked items can lead to personal liability.

ACCOUNTING REQUIREMENTS

The directors are responsible for keeping the company's books and records and preparing annual accounts. Audited accounts must be filed with the Registrar of Companies within ten months of the financial year end.

Details of these records are given in Table 7.4.

Table 7.3 (*Cont'd.*)

OTHER REQUIREMENTS

Generally directors must not use their position fo further their own interests at the company's expense. This involves a director:

1 Not receiving loans from the company unless approval is given in general meeting of the company and:
   (a) it is to meet company expenses; or
   (b) it enables him to properly perform his duties; or
   (c) it is in the ordinary course of the company's business
2 Disclosing his personal interest (including his spouse and children) in contracts with the company;
3 Not undertaking a substantial asset transaction with the company unless it is approved by the shareholders;
4 On departure obtaining shareholder approval for any compensation for loss of office.

Directors

Many people do not realize that the directors of even the smallest company have a long list of legal duties and responsibilities. The specific rules and limits of the powers by which they may manage the company are given in the Articles but there are many aspects of their general legal position which are not always understood. These are summarized in Table 7.3. This table is not intended to be an authoritative source of legal advice. For that you must consult a solicitor. But it is intended to be a helpful checklist of the major points. It should be studied with care as there is widespread ignorance of even some of the basic points.

It is particularly important to note that as a director of a company there are ways you can incur personal liability. The table draws attention to several ways a director may become personally liable for debts. Limited liability never extends to criminal acts of which he has knowledge.

Accounting Requirements

The Companies Acts require certain books and records to be kept by the directors. They also require the preparation of audited accounts for every financial year which, together with a director's report containing specified information, must be filed for public inspection at Companies House.

Table 7.4 summarizes the requirements which may seem complicated. Here is another instance of the value of a professional accountant being involved from the early days (he might, of course, be the auditor).

Subsequent Changes

The Memorandum and Articles of Association governing the activities and management of the company can be changed after incorporation. A share-holders' meeting is required. Certain other matters also require a shareholders' meeting. For some (such as an increase in authorized capital) an ordinary resolution (i.e. 50% of the votes or more) is sufficient. Other changes require a special resolution (75% of the votes or more). There are rules governing the length of notice given to shareholders of the meeting and the business which may be conducted at such meetings. It is always best to involve a professional (solicitor or accountant) in such matters as mistakes can be disastrous.

Changes in directors are governed by the Articles. The main rules are summarized in Table 7.3.

Changes in shareholders are a matter of agreement on the price at which the shares will change hands and a registration of the new shareholder in the company's records. For a private company this registration is usually restricted by the Articles. Common restrictions are the right of the directors to refuse to register a transfer or the obligation to offer the shares first to existing share-holders at the same price.

General Comments on Tax

It is not the intention in this book to discuss the details of tax. Even a careful reading of up-to-date and authoritative books on tax is not recommended as an alternative to using a good tax adviser. It is useful to understand a little about tax but it is such a specialized and constantly changing area that you should seek advice. If you are using a good firm of accountants they will be able to offer this support.

One of the principles of operating a business run for profit is to plan to minimize tax. This is tax avoidance and is an entirely legitimate and legal aim. However, tax evasion which is non-payment of tax that should be paid (for example, by the falsification of accounts) is illegal.

All professional advisers would recommend planning to minimize tax but this policy can be carried too far. One weakness sometimes seen in a businessman is an obsession to avoid all tax. The one guaranteed and easy way of tax avoidance is to run all activities at a loss. This is, of course, ridiculous because the commercial aim of making profit has been sacrificed to achieve the less important aim of paying no tax. Some tax planning comes close to this ludicrous example by structuring the business or its activities in a way that hinders the efficiency of the commercial process. One of the problems of a complex tax avoidance scheme is that while it may work now, it may produce serious problems later if the tax rules change. Another is that bad tax advice can produce a bigger liability than the one being avoided. You should try to avoid the trap of allowing the tax tail to wag the commercial dog. Tax is seldom anywhere near 100% in which case extra profit is generally worthwhile despite the tax to be paid. There is no doubt that some people devote too much time to

Table 7.4: Statutory Accounting Requirements

RECORDS REQUIRED (which are entrusted to the directors for safe keeping)

Register of shareholders
Register of major shareholders
Register of directors and secretaries
Register of directors' interests
Copies of directors' service contracts
Minutes of shareholders' meetings
Minutes of directors' meetings
Register of mortgages and charges
Accounting records

Most of these records, except for the accounting records, must be available for public inspection. The auditors will often keep the records for a small company.

ACCOUNTING RECORDS

These must show the company's transactions and its financial position. They must enable the directors to ensure the annual report and accounts can show a 'true and fair view' of the company's financial position.

CONTENT OF THE RECORDS

The records must include details of:

1 The company's assets and liabilities.
2 Sales and purchases (and the identities of buyer and seller – except for retailers).
3 Payments and receipts of cash (and why).
4 Stock at each financial year end.

LOOKING AFTER THE RECORDS

The records must:

1 be kept up to date;
2 give sufficient information for the directors to manage the business properly;
3 be in a suitable form to ease the safeguarding of the company's assets.

The directors must make sure the accounting records are kept safely.

ANNUAL ACCOUNTS

The directors have a duty to make sure the accounts are prepared for every financial year of the company in a proper form. The responsibility remains with the directors though they usually delegate the preparation to others.

The accounts must:

1 give a true and fair view of the profit (or loss) and the company's state of affairs;
2 comply with a detailed list of statutory requirements;
3 be audited by a properly qualified accountant;
4 be signed by two directors (after board approval);
5 be presented at the company's annual general meeting;
6 be filed with the Registrar of Companies.

tax avoidance and would be better off in after tax profit terms if they devoted more energy to making profits. Very few good businesses are guilty of this mistake.

While obtaining good tax advice is recommended, it is also sensible to learn some of the principles of tax. This should include basic allowances and when tax is due. There are a number of good books on this subject written at a layman's level and some reading is suggested: the Reading List gives suggestions.

Partnership Taxation

If you trade as a sole trader or as a partnership you will be taxed as self-employed. In a partnership, each partner is jointly liable for income tax on the whole of the profits (as with any other debt). However, each partner is assessed to tax on his share of taxable profit. The amount of tax he pays will depend on his personal circumstances. These include his personal allowances, life insurance premiums, mortgage interest relief on his home and so on.

Basically, you will be liable to income tax on the profits of the business without deduction of partners' drawings or salary. The expenses which can be deducted from income to calculate taxable profits are those which are incurred 'wholly and exclusively' for the purpose of trade. In addition to expenses which can be deducted there are a number of allowances which can be claimed. For example, depreciation of a fixed asset cannot in general be deducted as an expense. Instead, there are capital allowances which can be claimed. Table 7.5 gives a list of the main expenses which can be deducted and the main allowances which can be claimed.

Once taxable profit has been calculated you will have to pay income tax on it. The tax rates are the normal sliding scale that applies to all income tax payers. However, the timing of the payments is different. In general, you will not have to pay tax until the tax year (6 April one year to 5 April the next) after the tax year in which your accounting period (normally 12 months) ends. In other words the tax on the profit shown in your annual accounts for the year ended 30 June 1982 will not be payable until the 1983/4 tax year. This tax would normally be payable in two equal instalments on 1 July 1983 and 1 January 1984. You will see that the timing of your accounting date can affect the length of time before the tax needs to be paid. In general, an accounting date early in the tax year gives you maximum credit. However, professional advice is sensible as the actual choice may depend on the type of your business.

The only other tax matter which it is appropriate to mention here is relief for losses. This can be important as your new business may trade at a loss initially. Some of the simple rules are summarized in Table 7.5. You will see that, in general, losses can be set off against certain profits either past, present or future. One important tax advantage of starting trading as a partnership is that

Table 7.5: Expenses which can be Deducted in Calculating Taxable Profit and Allowances which can be Claimed by a Sole Trader or Partnership

EXPENSES

The general rule is that expenses 'wholly and exclusively' incurred in running the business are allowable. Others are not.

This is a list of what normally applies. There may be exceptions in specific cases. Also you should always check the up-to-date position because some of these rules will change. The references here are correct as at the end of 1982.

Expense	Allowable?	Comments
Costs of production, marketing, selling.	Yes	General costs of running the business are allowed just as in calculating profit with some exceptions noted below.
Costs of running the premises and other general overheads.	Yes	

The items which follow are commonly the cause of misunderstanding.

Advertising	Yes	
Wages, salaries	Yes	Includes bonuses, PAYE and the cost of fringe benefits for the employees *not* the partners.
Rent, rates etc.	Yes	Provided for business purposes.
Subscriptions.	Yes	If to trade or professional associations.
Donations.	Yes	Donations to charities are allowable provided there is a business or trading connection.
Travel and subsistence.	Yes/No	Only in the course of business activities. Travel between home and the business address is excluded.
Repairs and maintenance of premises/plant.	Yes/No	Repairs are allowable. Cost of additions, alterations or improvements are not (but capital allowances are possible – see below).
Telephone.	Yes	Business use only.
Entertainment.	No/Yes	Unless for staff or overseas customers.
Legal fees.	No/Yes	Not if incurred in acquiring an asset. But allowable if connected with maintaining an asset (e.g. chasing debtors).
Personal expenses.	No	
Depreciation.	No	But capital allowances may be claimed.

ALLOWANCES

Capital

Although depreciation is not generally allowed there are a number of exceptions where

Table 7.5 *(Cont'd.)*

---

the capital cost can be claimed in whole or part. The rules are complicated but in simple terms are:

Plant and machinery (including fixtures and fittings).	100% of cost may be claimed in the year of acquisition. This also applies to hire purchased but not leased assets.
Industrial buildings. (not offices or warehousing)	75% initial allowance in first year can be claimed, plus 4% of cost in that year. Then 4% in each later year until the cost is fully written off.
Agricultural land and buildings.	20% initial allowance in first year can be claimed plus 10% writing down allowance in that year. Then 10% can be claimed in each of the next 7 years.
Motor cars.	Only goods vehicles qualify for the 100% rule. 25% of the cost of the business' pool of cars (less amounts already claimed) can be claimed in each year provided each car costs less than £8,000. Otherwise the maximum is £2,000 on each car still showing at a cost of £8,000 or more after deducting allowances claimed to date.

---

losses in the first four years of trading can be offset against your income, including your salary, for the previous three years. This does not apply to a limited company.

Limited Company Taxation

A company has a separate legal existence from its shareholders. It will be taxed under corporation tax rather than income tax rules. The rate is usually a fixed percentage of profit (52% in recent years) unless profits are below a certain level when the 'small companies rate' applies (38% recently). Corporation tax is payable nine months after the end of the company's financial year.

The calculation of the taxable profits of a company is similar to a partnership. Table 7.6 lists the allowable expenses and allowances which can be claimed in a similar way to Table 7.5. Most of the differences are not great except for the treatment of directors and shareholders. In the case of a company, owners' salaries are deducted in calculating taxable profit. These salaries are then taxable under income tax rules in the normal way. In some circumstances it can be tax advantageous to draw all the profits as salary, pay income tax and lend the money back to the company.

Dividends deserve a brief mention. A company may decide to pay dividends on its shares (particularly if some shareholders do not draw a salary or directors' fees). These payments are made net of basic rate income tax (in a similar

Table 7.5 *(Cont'd.)*

Stock

Stock and work in progress	The increased value of the stock less £2,000 held on the last day of your previous accounts can be deducted from taxable profit. The increase is calculated by reference to a published All Stocks Index.

Losses

First four years trading.	Can be offset against other income (which includes your previous salary) of the preceding three years.
Set off of losses against other income.	Trading losses can be offset against other income in the same year of assessment or the following year (if the trade continues).
Carry forward of losses.	A claim above would give an immediate tax repayment. Instead you may carry the loss forward to set against later profits of the same trade without time limit.
Carry back of a terminal loss	A loss in the last 12 months of trading can be carried back to offset against the profits of the previous 3 years.

way to building society deposit interest). The company must, therefore, make a payment of 'Advanced Corporation Tax (ACT) equal to this basic rate tax to the Inland Revenue at the time of paying the dividend. The ACT payments can usually be deducted from the 'main stream' corporation tax bill which will, of course, not be paid until some months later.

Formal Registration Requirements

A number of registration requirements for a new business have already been mentioned. Table 7.7 brings together the points already mentioned, as well as some that have not, to give a reasonably complete list.

One important area which has not been mentioned in this chapter is insurance. Apart from National Insurance the only legal requirement is to take out Employer's Liability Insurance and prominently display the certificate. A reputable insurance broker can advise on this. However, you would be foolish to commence trading without other insurances. Table 7.8 gives a brief list of the main insurances to consider in your discussions with a good broker.

There are also other formalities which might be required in specific circumstances. These mostly concern your local authority or local representative of other bodies. They include planning permission, Factory Act regulations, effluent disposal and electricity for heavy power uses.

Table 7.6: Expenses which can be Deducted in Calculating Taxable Profit and Allowances which can be Claimed by a Company

---

EXPENSES

The general rule is that expenses 'wholly and exclusively' incurred in running the business are allowable. Others are not.

This is a list of what normally applies. There may be exceptions in specific cases. Also you should always check the up-to-date position because the rules change frequently. These references are up to date at at the end of 1982.

Expense	Allowable?	Comments
Costs of production, marketing, selling.	Yes	General costs of running the business are allowed just as in calculating profit with some exceptions noted below.
Costs of running the premises and other general overheads.	Yes	

The items which follow are commonly the cause of misunderstanding.

Advertising	Yes	
Wages, salaries	Yes	Includes bonuses, PAYE and the cost of fringe benefits for the employees including the owners.
Rent, rates etc.	Yes	Provided for business purposes.
Subscriptions.	Yes	If to trade or professional associations.
Donations.	Yes	Donations to charities are allowable provided there is a business or trading connection.
Travel and subsistence.	Yes/No	Only in the course of business activities. Travel between home and the business address is excluded.
Repairs and maintenance of premises/plant.	Yes/No	Repairs are allowable. Cost of additions, alterations or improvements are not (but capital allowances are possible – see below).
Telephone.	Yes	Business use only.
Entertainment.	No	Unless for staff or overseas customers.
Legal fees.	No/Yes	Not if incurred in acquiring an asset. But allowable if connected with maintaining an asset (e.g. chasing debtors).
Personal expenses.	No	
Depreciation.	No	But capital allowances may be claimed.

Table 7.6 (*Cont'd.*)

ALLOWANCES

Capital

Although depreciation is not allowed in general there are a number of exceptions where the capital cost can be claimed in whole or part. The rules are complicated but in simplest terms are:

Plant and machinery (including fixtures and fittings).	100% of cost may be claimed in the year of acquisition. This also applies to hire purchased but not leased assets.
Industrial buildings. (not offices or warehousing)	75% initial allowance in first year can be claimed, plus 4% of cost in that year. Then 4% in each later year until the cost is fully written off.
Agricultural land and buildings.	20% initial allowance in first year can be claimed plus 10% writing down allowance in that year. Then 10% can be claimed in each of the next 7 years.
Motor cars.	Only goods vehicles qualify for the 100% rule. 25% of the cost of the business' pool of cars (less amounts already claimed) can be claimed in each year provided each car costs less than £8,000. Otherwise the maximum is £2,000 on each car still showing at a cost of £8,000 or more after deducting allowances claimed to date.
Stock and work in progress	The increased value of the stock less £2,000 held on the last day of your previous accounts can be deducted from taxable profit. The increase is calculated by reference to a published All Stocks Index.

Losses

Use of losses.	Trading losses can be set against other profits of the same period including capital gains. Trading losses of one company in a group can be passed to another member.
Carry forward of losses.	Trading losses can be carried forward to set against future profits from the same trade.
Carry back of losses.	Trading losses can be carried back for one year and set against any trading profits of that year.
Capital allowances.	If a claim for capital allowances creates a loss for tax purposes this may be carried back for three years.
Terminal losses.	Trading losses incurred in the last twelve months of trading can be carried back for three years.

Employing People

The amount of current legislation about employing people is daunting. There are minimum legal standards in a wide range of different areas and employees have rights which must be respected. There is, too, a considerable administrative burden involved in all this. Remember that the general aim of the legal

Table 7.7: Formal Registration Requirements

What must be registered?	With whom?	Comments
Business Formation		
Limited partnership	Registrar of Companies	Otherwise partners liability not limited. See page 98
Limited company	Registrar of Companies	See page 98
Changes in company name	Registrar of Companies	See page 101
Tax		
Start of work as self employed (sole trader/ partnership)	Form 41G should be sent to local Inspector of Taxes. Also P45 from your last employer	See Inland Revenue brochure I.R. 28 *Starting in Business*
PAYE	Your local Inspector of Taxes should be told. He will supply details of how to deduct PAYE	See employers guide to PAYE – Inland Revenue pamphlet P7
VAT Consult your local VAT	office of the Customs and Excise	
Insurance		
National Insurance	Self employed traders must continue to pay to local tax office. As an employer there are employer's payments and employee deductions to account for	See DHSS leaflet NI41
Employers' liability insurance	Insure through a reputable broker	By law this insurance must be held and the certificate displayed
Other matters	Your local authority may need to be consulted on planning permission (which includes the use of a building) or other matters	

Table 7.8: Minimum Insurances to Consider

National Insurance	A legal requirement. See Table 7.8.
Employers liability	A legal requirement. See Table 7.8.
Personal injury	As a self employed man you will not be covered by National Health insurance should you be injured at work.
Key man insurance	Life and health insurance on the key individuals is wise in a new business.
Buildings and contents including stock	It would be foolish not to insure. Any lender will insist.
Loss of profits	A common form of insurance to cover the loss of income if the business is interrupted by, say, fire.
Product liability	A common protection against accident or injury to others resulting from your product being defective.
Credit insurance	Particularly valuable when exporting (usually through ECGD).

Table 7.9: Points to Remember when Employing People

Recruiting and Hiring

Sex and race	Jobs must be open to all. If you employ less than six people the sex discrimination rules do not normally apply.
Disabled people	If you employ 20 or more at least 3% must be registered disabled. If you cannot satisfy this you should consult your Jobcentre.
Contracts of employment	You must provide one in writing within 13 weeks of employing a person. See Table 7.10 for an example.
Wages	Some industries have statutory minimum rates. See your Jobcentre. Detailed payslips must be given covering deductions. You must pay employers', and deduct employees', National Insurance contributions.
Pensions	The Department of Health and Social Security can advise on the State Scheme.
Working hours	Some jobs such as driving have legal limits. Young people under 18 are also restricted.
Time off	Employees have the right to reasonable time off for:

antenatal clinic attendance (paid)
trade union work (unpaid)
public duties (unpaid)

A woman about to have a baby who (1) has worked for you for more than 2 years (2) works up to the eleventh

Table 7.9 (*Cont'd.*)

	week of pregnancy is entitled to 90% of her normal pay for six weeks and her job back (or an alternative) for up to 29 weeks after the birth if she follows certain rules.
Health and safety	Your premises may be inspected for safety. If you employ more than five people you must prepare a written health and safety statement. You must notify any major accidents via the Health and Safety Executive. You must take out employers liability insurance to cover your employees against accidents or disease at work. If industrial injury benefit is claimed by an employee you will need to fill in a DHSS form.
Training	An Industrial Training Board may be useful for advice and help. Consider a Group Training Association to share costs with others. The Training Services Division of the Manpower Services Commission can help.
Short time working or temporary lay off	You must pay a 'guarantee payment' if the employee has worked for more than four weeks. This amount is the daily amount the employee would expect subject to a maximum and is limited to five days in any three month period. If you use short time working to avoid ten or more redundancies you may qualify for help under the Department of Employment's Temporary Short-time Working Compensation Scheme.
Industrial ralations	An employee has a right to belong to a union. You might need to consider recognizing a union. You can seek help from ACAS.
Discipline and dismissals	The rules must be clear and well understood. Employees must have a copy. Full explanations and oral and written warnings must be given. An employee has a right to be accompanied by another employee at a disciplinary hearing. He has the right of appeal. If you dismiss someone who has worked for 26 weeks or more they have a right to a written explanation within 14 days. The employee must be paid during his minimum period of notice. Employees can complain to an Industrial Tribunal within three months if they have been employed for more than one year.
Redundancy	If you wish to make ten or more redundancies you must notify the Department of Employment at least 30 days before. If you recognize a trade union you must go through a consultation procedure. If employees have less than two years service they are not entitled to redundancy payments. Otherwise a lump sum depending on age and service is payable. The Department of Employment will tell you the legal minimum. 41% of the cost of minimum redundancy payments can be re-claimed.

controls is to ensure that employers carry out their responsibilities towards employees. Good working relationships is one of the most important aspects of any successful business. If you do the job of hiring, paying, training and managing people properly they will respect you for it and reward your efforts with loyalty. Indeed, it is astonishing how loyal the employees of a small business can be (in contrast to some big companies). It is common to hear them say that they know they are important to its success and will accept the risks in return for the feeling of being wanted.

Recruiting and Conditions of Employment

It was mentioned in Chapter 3, page 32, and is emphasized on page 146, that the right staff is vital if a new business is to succeed. Therefore, you will need to recruit with care, using professional help where necessary. Sources of help are you local Jobcentre and, for some posts, professional recruitment agencies. There are rules concerning sex and race discrimination and the employment of disabled people which are summarized in Table 7.9.

Having decided you wish to employ somebody you have to decide what wage or salary you will offer. In some industries there are statutory minimum wages but you are more likely to be affected by the going rate in the area. You may decide you will pay the minimum salary you can to recruit someone. Or you may prefer to pay a premium rate to get a good person. A useful maxim is 'if you pay peanuts, expect to employ monkeys'. By employing good, well paid and motivated people you will probably finish up with a lower total wage bill, because of higher productivity, than you would get with a poor workforce.

Once salary or wages are agreed and the recruit is hired you must, within thirteen weeks, provide him or her with a written statement of the main terms and conditions of employment. An example of a statement is given in Table 7.10 which is quoted from the Department of Industry's Small Firms Service booklet on employing people.

There are a large number of regulations about matters such as the maximum hours a driver can work, health and safety, short time working, the position if a woman employee becomes pregnant and so on. Some of these are summarized in Table 7.9. You should read the booklet mentioned above and consult your local Jobcentre/Employment office for further details. Appendix 2 lists other sources of help.

Training

You will need to be sure all your employees are properly trained to do their work well. Even those who are experienced may need to adjust to your needs and a short training programme may be sensible.

In the longer term you will need to organize training for new recruits, particularly the younger ones. Your company may be within the scope of an

Industrial Training Board. They can help you and provide advice and information on grants and levys. It may be useful to join a Group Training Association. This is an arrangement to share the costs and administration of training with other firms. Finally, the Training Services Division of the Manpower Services Commission may be able to provide training facilities tailored to suit your needs.

Industrial Relations

Good industrial relations will be very important if you want an effectively-run business. Good communications are an important part of this. Not only should employees be fully aware of the company's rules but you should try to tell them as much as possible about the running of it. This will help their sense of identity with the business and its success.

Unions are often a sore point with small companies. You may find your employees wish to be union represented though this is often not the case in a small company. You should certainly consider the strength of employee feeling on the subject and it is illegal to prevent an employee belonging to a union. If you have difficulties or queries you can call upon the services of ACAS (the Advisory Conciliation and Arbitration Service). The Department of Employment publishes useful Codes of Practice on this and related topics.

Discipline, Dismissal and Redundancy

The first principle of good discipline is to have clearly understood and sensible rules which are agreed with your employees (and unions if appropriate). It is important to lay down the procedure to follow if there is a problem.

You must give full explanations at all stages if an employee is criticised. There must be a chance of reply and a right to be accompanied at any disciplinary meeting. There should also be a right of appeal. A proper dismissal procedure should involve oral and written warnings before action is taken unless, say, criminal acts have been involved. You will need to keep careful records and must give a minimum period of notice. The employee can make a complaint of unfair dismissal to an Industrial Tribunal in certain circumstances. If your procedures are clear and carefully followed you should not be faced with this problem.

Redundancy is fundamentally different from dismissal. It arises from your inability to keep a person employed rather than inadequate performance. The rules are therefore different and should be checked with the Department of Employment. You may have to give notice to the Department of Employment and consult with the unions involved. Redundancy payments must be made (accompanied by a written statement) and the minimum requirements are briefly listed in Table 7.9. Some of this cost can be recovered from the Department of Employment.

116

Table 7.10: An Example of a Possible Form for use as a Written Statement under the Employment Protection (Consolidation) Act 1978

WRITTEN STATEMENT OF MAIN TERMS AND CONDITIONS OF EMPLOYMENT

Part I of this statement sets out particulars of the terms and conditions on which I (name of employer) am employing you (name of employee) on (date on which statement is issued).

Part II of this statement sets out information on disciplinary rules, whom you should contact if you wish to appeal against a disciplinary decision or to take up a grievance, and the subsequent steps to be followed in the disciplinary and grievance procedures.

* Your employment with me began on (date) and, by virtue of paragraph 17 or 18 of Schedule 13 to the above Act, your previous employment with (name of previous employer or employers) counts as part of you continuous period of employment which therefore began on (date continuous period of employment commenced).

* Your employment with me began on (date). Your employment with your previous employer does not count as part of your continuous period of employment.

Part I

1   You are employed as a (insert job title).

2   Pay will be (insert scale or rate of remuneration, or the method of calculating remuneration and intervals at which remuneration is to be paid).

3   Hours of work are (give normal hours and any other related terms and conditions).

4   Holidays and holiday pay (give sufficient details to enable entitlement, including accrued holiday pay, to be precisely calculated).

5   Incapacity for work (state terms and conditions relating to sickness or injury and sick pay – if none, say so).

6   Pensions and pension schemes (state terms and conditions or refer to relevant handbook or other document which is reasonably accessible to the employee – if none, say so).

7   Amount of notice of termination to be given by:

(a) the employer is (insert period);
(b) the employee is (insert period).

Fixed-term contracts should state date of expiry instead.

* Delete as appropriate.

Part II

1   The disciplinary rules which apply to you in your employment are (explain them).

or

the disciplinary rules which apply to you in your employment can be found in (reference should be made to a handbook or other document which is given to the employee with the written statement and additional note, or, if that is not practicable, can be read by the employee in a place to which access can be gained without difficulty).

2   If you are dissatisfied with any disciplinary decision which affects you, you should appeal in the first instance to (name of the employee to whom the appeal should be made or the position held, for example supervisor).

Table 7.10 *(Cont'd.)*

3   You should make your appeal by (explain how appeals should be made).

or

The way in which appeals should be made is explained in (refer to an accompanying handbook or a document which is reasonably accessible to the employee).

4   If you have a grievance about your employment you should apply in the first instance to (give the name of the employee with whom the grievance should be raised or the position held, for example personnel officer).

5   You should explain your grievance by (explain how grievances are to be raised).

or

The way in which grievances should be raised is explained in (refer again to an accompanying handbook or, if necessary, a document which is reasonably accessible to the employee).

6   Subsequent steps in the firm's disciplinary and grievance procedures are (explain them).

or

Details of the firm's disciplinary and grievance procedures are set out in (refer to an accompanying handbook or, if necessary, another document which is reasonably accessible to the employee).

Note: These separate stages can of course be telescoped where, for example, the same person is the first to be approached for appeals against disciplinary decisions and for grievances, or where the method of application for both is the same.

7   A contracting-out certificate under the Social Security Pensions Act 1975 is/is not* in force for the employment in respect of which this written statement is being issued.

* Delete as appropriate.

Reprinted from the Department of Industry's Small Firms Service booklet entitled Employing People.

8

Controlling Your Business

Introduction

There are many books which deal in depth with the problems of controlling a business. It is not the intention of this chapter to try to cover the subject completely in a few pages. However, it is hoped to give you an insight into the basic necessities and an introduction to the standard approaches of financial control. It has already been mentioned that financial control is the most common weakness of small companies. This cannot be emphasized too strongly as companies more commonly fail when they run out of cash than for any other reason. This is why the brief discussions in this chapter will mostly be concerned with the control of finance. People, their control and motivation, are also so important to a small business that they, too, are discussed. It should be recognized, however, that control of other aspects of the business such as production, marketing and research and development should not be neglected but are beyond the scope of this book. The habits of control should be acquired early as your new business is most likely to fail in its first year or so when money will be tightest and there are no reserves of customer, supplier or staff goodwill to draw on.

No company is likely to be properly controlled unless it has some sort of plan of what is to be attempted during, say, the next year against which it can compare progress. This plan is of little value if the management do not meet regularly to discuss progress and decide on any corrective action that may be needed. Many small companies do not even have regular management meetings (or board meetings) on the grounds that they are too busy or everybody meets frequently enough anyway. This is a mistake as a regular formal meeting with an agreed agenda is probably the best way of keeping all important people informed of the progress in areas which are not their direct responsibility. It also ensures general commitment to decisions made by the meetings. In a new, one-man company there are, of course, no people to meet at first and this is no doubt why many such companies fail to have proper meetings even when the company is no longer small. The problem of adjusting to growth is discussed further in Chapter 11.

Minimum Records to Keep

Even the simplest business must keep financial records which are good enough to enable proper accounts to be prepared. A limited company has to have its accounts audited and a partnership has to make acceptable returns to the tax man. In addition, the VAT system requires proper records which will have to be presented to the Customs and Excise every three months. Most importantly, however, no business can be properly controlled if it does not record financial matters in a way that allows it to see where it has got to. When an accountant is not employed, the auditors can easily and cheaply produce monthly management accounts from properly kept books.

In its early days, your new business is unlikely to need the large number of books which a full accounting system may demand. However, it makes sense not just to record all transactions in one big book. This makes analysis hard and chasing of debtors, for example, becomes difficult because their names are lost in the general confusion. Specially printed books which will help with layout and clarity can be purchased from any large stationery shop. It will probably make sense to employ a bookkeeper (possibly only part-time) to make up the books but this is not essential if they are written up systematically and frequently.

The essential books cover cash, wages, purchases and stock. Many businesses will, of course, have a more complex range of books than those mentioned below.

Cash Books

You will need to carefully record all cash transactions. It is common to keep two cash records.

Firstly, a bank account book which records all cash receipts and their payments into the bank. All withdrawals are also recorded whether cheque, standing order or direct debits. This book mainly serves to keep control of payments in and out of the bank of which cash will only be part. The book keeps a check on the level of cash (or overdraft) in the bank which is a vital piece of control information.

Secondly, a petty cash book will be needed. This records all payments into or out of the float of cash kept in the office to make small cash payments. These might include minor stationery purchases, some salesmen's expenses and postage costs.

Wages Book

You will need to keep a record of all wages and salaries paid. This record must show gross income, deductions for tax, National Insurance and pension contributions leading to a net pay figure. It should also show the employer's National

Insurance contributions. Table 7.7 gives details of where to obtain help with these calculations.

Sales

A common system to record sales which you might use involves two books. The first – the sales day book – records all sales invoices when issued. The second – the sales ledger – lists sales under customer names. The value of the second book is that it makes chasing debtors easier because sales (and whether they have been settled) are recorded under the right heading for this. It is, of course, possible to manage a simple business with only the one book which records all invoices, their date of issue and date of settlement.

Purchases

A common system to record purchases is similar to the sales system, namely a day book for recording invoices received and a ledger under supplier names. The argument for the second book is, again, to make the control of payments to particular suppliers easier. The purchases day book can be analysed with columns to note into what category each purchase falls. This can cover carriage, heat and light, rent, rates, capital expenditure and so on. Each column can then be totalled when management accounts are prepared.

Stock

Almost any business needs to keep careful records of stock held. If there are many different items the recording can be complicated but there are a number of excellent recording systems on the market. These usually keep a running total of the stock of each item together with re-order levels and amounts.

Minimum Control Information

There is nothing better for financial control purposes than regular management accounts linked to a budgetary control system and this should be an early aim. Even if your new business is not able to afford an accountant your auditors should be happy to prepare regular management accounts for you. However, it is recognized that many businesses do not use this service. This section, therefore, considers the minimum information you will need to avoid being completely in the dark if you do no formal budgetary or management accounting.

The vital items of financial information which you will need to know about your business are:

Table 8.1: The Minimum Information the Management Needs

The order position

A profit forecast and some information on actual results (e.g. sales)

A cash forecast and actual results

Some cost information

The stock position

Some staff performance information

Some information on the ability to fulfil orders

---

1 Is the business profitable? Are its separate activities profitable or not?
2 Will it continue to make profits (or losses) over the next few months?
3 What is the cash position now?
4 How will the cash position alter over the next few months?

Table 8.1 gives a summarized list of the minimum items of information which ought to be available to you. These will go some way towards answering all the above questions. The weakness will be in the profit area because of the lack of proper profit and loss accounts.

The Order Position

The order position will help you to prepare the sales forecast which is needed for your forecasts of profit and cash. It will also help you to forecast production levels and other activities which will be needed to fulfil the orders.

The best way of recording the information on orders is to compare it with the previous month and the position of a year ago. Table 8.2 gives a simple example. While the order position should be recorded in cash terms it may also be useful to prepare the information on a product by product basis to highlight trends which the overall figures might hide.

In the example it can be seen that the business is on average now delivering at approximately the rate it receives orders, i.e. the order book will not be changing much. Last year it was taking orders at a roughly 25% lower rate and was on average only delivering about two-thirds of the rate of order intake i.e. the order position was growing. Clearly, the company has not only improved its order intake compared with a year ago but has greatly improved its ability to fulfil orders.

Profit and Cash Forecasts

The use of cash forecasting is the best way of improving financial control in any small business. A profit forecast is also of great value because it gives a guide to the vital question of whether the business will be profitable, and by how much,

Table 8.2: An Example of an Order Position Summary

	THIS YEAR			LAST YEAR		
	This Month	Cumulative Position	Average Per Month	This Month	Cumulative Position	Average Per Month
Orders Received (A)	20,000	61,000	20,300	15,000	45,000	15,000
Orders Cancelled (B)	1,000	2,000	700	500	1,000	300
Deliveries (C)	26,000	62,000	20,700	8,000	30,000	10,000
Orders Carried Forward (= Orders Carried Forward From Last Month + A − B − C)	85,000			53,000		

123

over the next few months. They are mentioned together here because it is common to derive the cash forecast from a profit forecast. They have both been discussed at length in Chapter 4.

Having prepared profit and cash forecasts to validate your original business plan, you are in a good position to use them to help control the business. If you do not, the original work will have been partly wasted. For your forecasts to be of real use they must be reviewed frequently and extended as time passes. A common period for review is quarterly with another quarter's forecast added to replace the one past. It is important to check and revise the assumptions you made before you had any experience of running the business. The most important assumption to review is the forecast level of sales. The order position mentioned above and trading to date will now make this an easier task. Other assumptions such as credit taken from suppliers and given to customers will have a strong bearing on the cash position. All of this needs careful re-examination as you continue the forecasting exercise.

To use the forecasts for control purposes you need to compare actual results with your forecast for that period and highlight the main differences as a guide to where action is needed. Even without management accounts some simple checks against the cash forecast are possible. Table 8.3 gives an example of this with notes on the reasons for differences. These differences can then be discussed at the regular management meeting. This procedure is similar to that used in a proper budgetary control system and is discussed again on page 128.

Cost Information

It is not intended to discuss costing in detail here as this is a large subject on which many books have been written. In some businesses it is relatively easy. These are usually service companies such as retailers where little or no processing of bought-in stock is done. In others it can be very difficult. Manufacturing companies involved in large one-off projects are an example of this.

Basically, you will need to estimate the cost of producing and delivering product, however crudely, if you are to have a good idea of whether selling prices will lead to a profit. These costs will include:

Raw materials or bought-in stock
Labour
Advertising and selling costs
Delivery costs
General overheads of the premises
Finance costs.

As the level of activity in the business changes, cost per product unit will change. For example, as the factory gets more fully used the proportion of general overheads per unit product will tend to drop. This will reduce the cost per unit product. In addition, in times of inflation, many costs will change with time even if the level of activity does not change. These are the reasons for keeping the subject under close review.

For the purpose of analysis, costs are usually divided into two categories, namely variable and fixed costs (also known as direct and indirect costs). Variable costs change directly with the level of output. Raw material used is a good example. Labour, which is often thought of as a variable cost, may not be because people cannot be employed or laid off easily. Fixed costs do not change with output levels. They include rent and rates.

There are some problems with certain standard approaches of which you should be aware. It has already been seen that production costs vary with volume because the fixed costs of the factory and plant are divided between more units of output. Often companies ignore this by adding a fixed percentage to labour to cost the product (with the aim of recovering fixed costs). This can give misleading results. Another approach some companies choose is to allocate fixed costs by product line. This can give a broad feel for the overhead recovery each area must produce but it too can be misleading because of arbitrary allocation. Also, a manager's performance is then less easily highlighted. This is because many of the costs he is notionally incurring are outside his control and his actions on those he does control appear less significant than they may be. A further problem with this approach is that the individual managers naturally feel no responsibility for costs they cannot control while the central management, having allocated fixed costs, tends to lose incentive to control them; so nobody does.

You may have realized from some of the earlier comments that costing can become overcomplicated and lose value just by its complexity. One approach you can relatively easily adopt even in the earliest stages of your new business is to classify costs as fixed or variable. For example, fixed costs will include rent, finance, many labour costs and general overheads. Examples of variable costs are materials, subcontract manufacturing, sales commissions and distribution costs. This classification will allow you to see how much each extra unit of sales will cost (just the variable costs). The business will then break even when the total gross profit (sales income less variable costs) just covers the fixed costs. After this, the gross profit on each extra sale will directly add to net profit because fixed costs have already been covered. This approach is crude because costs do not all easily break down into these two categories. However, it gives a useful feel for what is happening and whether or not a particular sale is profitable. For example, provided fixed costs are already covered any sale at a price above the variable costs makes a contribution to profit (or a marginal profit as it is often called). This may justify some product lines or special price deals on which the business could not survive if other sales had not covered fixed costs. Clearly any sale below variable costs should be avoided.

Stock Position

You should always aim to keep a close check on stocks. Too much means money tied up needlessly and expensively. Too little may hinder your ability to deliver on time. The ideal is to always have the minimum stock consistent with delivery on time. Other factors to take note of include:

1 Can suppliers be relied upon? Or should some extra stock be held in case deliveries are late?
2 Bulk buying discounts may make it worthwhile to hold larger stocks.

A frequent review of the raw material and finished goods stock levels with these criteria in mind should be made. Additional information should include a note of customers being kept waiting beyond the delivery date quoted and the

Table 8.3: A Comparison of the Forecast Cash Position for a Particular Period with Achievement

QUARTER 1 1983

	Forecast A	Actual B	Variance B − A	Reason	Action Needed
Receipts					
Debtors	15,000	13,300	(1,700)	(a) Lower sales (b) Debtors slow to pay	More sales effort Better credit control
VAT	2,300	1,800	(500)	Lower purchases	Reflects lower sales
Sale of Assets	1,500	—	(1,500)	No buyer found yet	Advertise at a lower price
Total Received (A)	£18,800	£15,100	(£3,700)		
Payments					
Purchases	5,200	4,100	(1,100)	Lower sales	
VAT	3,100	2,900	(200)	Lower sales	
Wages/Salaries	10,100	10,500	400	Error in forecast	Check figures better
Capital Expenditure	1,000	1,200	200	Underestimated cost	
Interest	500	600	100	Bank rate rise	
Total Payments (B)	£19,900	£19,300	(£600)		
Cash Movement	(£1,100)	(£4,200)	(£3,100)		

levels of goods returned as unsatisfactory. The latter will give clues about the quality control of the business and needs to be watched carefully.

Staff Performance

At the very least you will need to monitor staff costs compared with turnover. Increases in the costs relative to turnover will eventually turn profits to losses. It may be that prices need to increase to cover increased staff costs or that overmanning has developed. Alternatively, too much overtime might be the problem; this cost needs frequent review.

Every employee in the business should be set targets against which to judge his effectiveness. In your new business any weak member of staff can hazard the existence of the whole company. This is particularly true of managers and supervisors.

The Ability to Fulfil Orders

As sales grow you will need to frequently review your ability to fulfil orders. A growing order book may seem healthy but it can also indicate an inability to produce and deliver goods at the levels required.

The capacity to fulfil orders may be adversely affected by something fundamental like a factory that is too small, too little machinery, too few skilled staff. Or it may be affected by something easier to correct like a shortage of packing material.

Sometimes this review will lead to recruitment of new staff and improvements in general operating procedures. Sometimes, if the business is growing, it will lead to a major decision on further capital investment.

Budgeting

Although survival is likely to be the keynote in the early days of your new business, this book has urged the need to do some planning and strategic thinking from the beginning. If this has been done properly before starting you will have formed good habits which will not be forgotten once your business is trading. We have discussed predicting the progress of the business with profit and cash forecasts and recognized the many difficulties of doing this. If you have followed this advice you will be one important step ahead of the average small businessman who does not plan or forecast on the grounds of either 'I haven't the time' or 'with so many uncertainties around how can my forecasts be accurate?'. Any growing business faces both of these problems but can prepare forecasts which take some account of the range of possibilities for uncertainties such as the rate of inflation.

Forecasts and Budgets

We can now discuss one of the most important of all modern management control techniques, namely budgetary control. First you need to be aware that a forecast differs conceptually from a budget. A forecast is the best estimate of future performance. A budget expresses the annual plan in cash terms so that each member of management has a tool to help him achieve the plan (and against which performance can be monitored). The budget is thus part of the management's means of control of the performance of the business.

Simple Budgeting

The word 'plan' has been used deliberately in the previous paragraph because a company can, of course, alter its destiny considerably by planning its course of action. The word 'forecast' implies a more passive approach to predicting the future without trying to affect it. However, in practice the two words are often used as alternatives to describe the company's short-term plans which will, of course, reflect predictions of changes in the outside environment. Often, the process of planning for the next 12 months will first involve a draft forecast of what will happen if no drastic changes are made. In a time of recession, for example, this may indicate an impending cash crisis. Action must then be discussed so that, ideally, a plan is developed which leads to a forecast profit. This may then be the adopted plan which could involve much physical change such as the lay-off of staff, the selling of assets and other drastic changes. Once all are agreed the plan can be adopted in the form of detailed budgets for each manager.

In its simplest form, budgeting only involves preparing forecasts based on the adopted plan for the year and subsequently comparing these forecasts with actual results as a guide to action. This should help you either (i) bring the business back to its forecast path or (ii) alter the forecasts to take account of revised assumptions (e.g. the assumed annual inflation rate might have been 10% and now looks like 20%).

Table 8.3, which was discussed earlier, is a simple example of budgetary control. You can see that actual results are compared with the forecast cash position and explanations given in note form. Corrective action is also proposed where necessary. Some differences such as the error in the wages calculation from forecast are trivial. Some such as the sales shortfall are more fundamental and corrective action will need greater effort.

If your company is very small forecasts for the overall company operations, such as were discussed in Chapter 4, will be adequate for budgetary control. However, if your new business is not tiny, or grows quickly, it will be necessary to break down these forecasts on a divisional or functional basis. As soon as one man is not responsible for all the company's activities it is necessary to assign responsibility for the budgetary control of each activity to the person who is responsible for that activity.

128

Full Budgetary Control

Table 8.4 summarizes the stages required for a full budgetary control system. It will be seen that the key is for the company to know what it wants to achieve in the budgetary period (say 12 months), to decide who should do what to achieve this aim and who is responsible for correcting deviations from each part of the plan. You will see that overall plans must be broken down to assign specific responsibilities to particular individuals. Table 8.5 is an illustration of this breakdown using the example of a company's overhead expenses.

It is not the intention of this section to discuss the details of budgetary control more fully. For that, the Reading List in Appendix 3 gives some suggestions. However, you should be aware that budgetary control is a universally recognized management tool in use in larger companies. It takes time to set up, review regularly, and use; but its benefits are enormous. This particularly applies to any business where the managing director cannot deal with all the company's problems and must delegate to other managers. He can then judge their performance against figures which they originally proposed or at least agreed to accept. If you decide not to adopt this approach at an early stage you should review the position regularly as the time will come when you will not easily be able to manage without it.

Although budgeting has great benefits it does have snags. The main one is that for it to work properly each individual must at least accept his budget even if he does not propose it. This may well lead to conflict as, for example, the sales director may say he will sell 10,000 units but the production director says he can only make 7,500. Such conflicts need to be reconciled in management meetings, under the control of the managing director who is concerned with the overall plan. Ideally, the reconciliation needs to be acceptable to all if full commitment is to be achieved.

Table 8.4: The Stages Needed for a Full Budgetary Control System

1   A clear organizational structure must be established.

2   Authority must be delegated to each manager. He must know what he is responsible for and how far his authority extends.

3   The company must have an overall objective, at least for the period of the budgets, leading to a corporate plan of action.

4   Budgets, based on the plans, must be prepared in conjunction with the individuals responsible for each activity to be budgeted.

5   A feedback system is needed to provide information on actual results which can be compared with the budgets.

6   The feedback information must be used to correct changes and to make new plans where necessary.

Table 8.5: An Example of a Company's Overhead Expenses Allocated to Specific Managers for Budgetary Control Purposes

Overheads	Total	Managing Director	Sales Director	Production Director	Development Manager	Accountant
	£	£	£	£	£	£
Factory	125,000			125,000		
Maintenance	15,500			15,500		
Buying Department	12,000			12,000		
Transport	14,000			14,000		
Stores	16,500			16,500		
Production Engineering	15,000			15,000		
R and D	10,500				10,500	
Sales	51,000		51,000			
Administrative Costs	130,000					130,000
Canteen	11,000					11,000
Finance Charges	13,500					13,500
Management Costs	41,000	41,000				
Personnel Department	10,500	10,500				
TOTALS	£465,500	£51,500	£51,000	£198,000	£10,500	£154,500

Note

This is only an illustrative example. In practice it may well be, for example, that the production director is not responsible for the factory. What is important, however, is that all the overheads are allocated to particular individuals who will then be responsible for them.

Corrective Action

A budgetary control system is useless if you do not take corrective action when it is needed. The first step is to discuss reports on progress against budget (such as Table 8.3) at management meetings. These meetings need not all involve everybody; for example, some may just be the managing director with one department head. Part of the importance of them is that more general problems can be uncovered in discussion. For example, referring back to Table 8.3, the wages calculation error looks trivial. However, similar errors may have occurred in other recent reports and the competence of the person preparing the reports may need to be questioned. Perhaps, too, there are other graver errors which have not yet come to light. In the Table 8.3 example, the most worrying error seems to be the shortfall in sales which will probably start to undermine the whole budget for the year and, indeed, may ultimately threaten the company's survival. All the present budget report tells the management is that sales are too low. They now need to ask why before deciding on corrective action. At one extreme this action may be more effort from the salesmen, at the other extreme it may mean cutting back on overheads to adjust to lower sales levels than originally budgeted.

You will now appreciate that corrective action (both its discussion and implementation) is not only the most important part of the budgetary process but is also the most time-consuming and difficult. It is what managing a business in financial terms is all about. It is the means by which the business is steered on to its chosen path rather than allowed to wander freely.

Finally, remember the importance of producing the budget reports as early as possible after the end of the period. Any time lost here is time lost before corrective action can be taken. It may also mean that the corrective action implied by the report is now not correct because of subsequent changes. Also as another reason for speed, the figures may indicate an impending cash crisis. In such circumstances, it is vital to have the earliest possible warning if there is to be time to find a solution. This is discussed further on page 159.

Management Accounts

The previous section referred to the value of feedback on the actual performance of the business which can be used as a guide to corrective action when compared with the forecast. This enables control to be achieved. What form then should this feedback take? Ideally, it should include up-to-date information on all budgeted items throughout the company. This is not easy to achieve without proper recording systems which will involve considerable accountancy support. As a principle, it is better to have quick, approximate information (within, say, ten days of the end of the month) than slow accurate information or corrective action will always be made much later than needed. However, the ideal is to aim towards a full set of comparative information in the form of proper monthly management accounts. The management can then receive monthly profit and cash flow information which is broken down under budgeted headings.

The sooner some system of management accounting exists the better you will be in a position to monitor your progress. All but the very simplest new businesses should consider doing this from the outset. A professional investor may insist on it anyway. As your business can probably not justify the cost of a full-time accountant initially it is likely that in the early days the auditors will be needed to make up the books and then prepare these accounts. Even without the full adoption of budgetary control, you can then monitor your general progress against forecast and make corrective decisions long before the need might otherwise become apparent. This is a vital protective measure if your new business is to survive the first year or so.

Table 8.6 gives a blank form example of one useful layout for management accounts. This shows the gross profit, or contribution, separately for each of a range of products. Total contributions are then compared to total overheads to calculate profit. Comparisons of performance with both forecast and the prior year's results for the same period are given. This approach can give you valuable information about the strengths and weaknesses of the performance. For example, some products may be loss-making despite profits being achieved overall. Again, although each product may be contributing to profitability this may be less than a year ago. These are instances where action is likely to be necessary to improve performance in later periods.

Credit Control

Credit control is the process of controlling cash payments and collecting cash due and needs the closest attention even in the smallest company. Many companies find themselves in difficulties because of weak credit control leading to bad debts (i.e. their credit risk assessment is poor and customers do not pay their bills) or late payments (i.e. cash collection is poor and customers pay late). This section gives a brief introduction to the most important areas of credit control. You should also be aware of the need to protect your assets against theft. Careful custody of cash is one obvious need as is the careful control of stock losses from theft.

Credit Control of Sales – Cash Business

If all your customers pay cash and goods do not change hands until the cash does, control is not difficult. However, most cash businesses accept cheques and credit cards which can lead to credit risks. Since the advent of cheque cards, a cheque has become a fairly safe form of cash. However, staff must be trained to check the system is used correctly and all such cards only guarantee a cheque to a certain limit. Credit cards also require staff training but have the advantage that higher levels of payment can be safely accepted once telephoned sanction has been obtained from the credit card centre.

Table 8.6: An Example of a Profit and Loss Account Showing the Contribution to Profit from Separate Products

RESULTS FOR MONTH Y OF 198X

	MONTH			CUMULATIVE (for year to date)		
	Actual %	*Budget* %	*Prior* % Year	*Actual* %	*Budget* %	*Prior* % Year
SALES						
Product A						
B						
C						
DIRECT COSTS						
Product A						
B						
C						
CONTRIBUTION						
Product A						
B						
C						
OVERHEADS						
Factory						
Sales						
Administration						
Directorate						
Finance Costs						
NET PROFIT						
Breakeven Sales Level						

(Total Contributions equal Total Overheads)

Table 8.7: Control Points for an Invoice Credit System

CREDIT RISK REDUCTION	*Notes*
1 Do a company search.	Organizations such as Dun and Bradstreet and UAPT can provide this service.
2 Take trade references.	Particularly from other suppliers to the company.
3 Do not allow high levels of credit to a customer until experience of the account has been gained.	One big bad debt can kill a new company.
4 Consider credit insurance where appropriate.	ECGD do this cheaply for export risks.
GENERAL CREDIT CONTROL POINTS	
1 Consider sending regular statements to reduce excuses for delay.	Many delays are due to petty errors.
2 Make sure you invoice whenever goods are supplied.	Speed of invoicing is needed if speed of collection is required.
3 Avoid any one debtor becoming so large its failure would hazard your business.	
4 All debtors need chasing occasionally. Some need constant reminding.	
5 Chasing by personal contact (e.g. telephone) usually works better than a letter.	The more persistent the debtor, the more persistent the chaser needs to be.
6 Discounts can be offered as an incentive to pay early.	Be careful. This can be expensive. A 5% discount for paying one month early is equivalent to an annual interest rate of 60%.
7 Have a formal system of regular financial reporting.	This should be discussed in management meetings when action can be decided.
IF PAYERS ARE REALLY DIFFICULT	
1 Stop supplying until payment is made.	Small companies are often scared of doing this to the bigger company.
2 A personal visit may produce results.	The extra embarrassment or aggravation is the key.
3 If the customer is in real trouble try and negotiate extended payment terms.	A writ may cause his collapse and your complete loss.
4 If the debt remains unpaid serve a writ through your solicitor.	This is a drastic action and costs money.
5 Early warning signs of trouble can be spotted by, say, your salesmen who should report back any such signs.	

The main problems with credit control in this type of business are the scope for human error and the ease with which cash can be stolen. This usually means good training is needed. Also one member of staff should be responsible for handling and looking after the cash collection. The system should include proper security for the cash and daily banking of it. If a till system is used, many modern ones have recording systems which minimize the danger of cash theft by staff because of the ability to check cash against sales receipts.

Credit Control of Sales – Invoice Business

The issue of a sales invoice and the giving of credit is a system common throughout business life. The amount of credit you offer will probably be dictated by the general terms in your industry but may sometimes be nego-tiated separately with different customers. Your credit controller will be con-cerned with three main problems:

1 Is the customer creditworthy? And for how much?
2 Do customers pay on time?
3 Are there disputes over amounts owing because of poorly prepared invoices or other reasons?

Table 8.7 gives a list of control points which are relevant to even the simplest invoice credit system.

Once you have established a control system you should monitor its perfor-mance. In particular, you will need to highlight the debts which are most in need of chasing. Table 8.8 gives a blank form for a simple breakdown of aged

Table 8.8: A Form for an Aged Debtor Report

Company Name	Credit Limit	Total Outstanding	Current	Over 30 Days	Over 60 Days	Notes/ Proposals for Action
TOTAL		(100%)	(%)	(%)	(%)	**Average** Debtor Period = ...days
Same Period Last Year		(100%)	(%)	(%)	(%)	**Average** Debtor Period = ...days

debtors, i.e. it lists each debt in age categories. This pattern can be compared with the same period in the previous year. The trend from month to month is a useful indicator of either the changing performance of the credit control or the changing pattern of customers' behaviour. When a particular customer moves out of line with the rest it indicates possible trouble and should be investigated.

Table 8.9: Control Points for a Purchasing System

SELECTING SUPPLIERS	*Notes*
1 Are the products of the necessary quality?	Returns by your customers will cause you major embarrassment and are costly.
2 Are the products available in the quantities required?	
3 Will delivery be made reliably on agreed dates?	A common problem.
4 What is the time interval between order and delivery?	This can vary enormously.
5 How much credit will the supplier give?	Price and credit are likely to be linked. Your new business may get no credit.
6 What is the price and how does it compare with competitors?	
CONTROL OF PAYMENTS TO SUPPLIERS	
1 No invoice should be paid until the department receiving the product is satisfied with it.	This might involve, say, satisfactory commissioning of a piece of new equipment.
2 Payment should preferably be against statements not individual invoices.	This makes control easier.
3 Statements should be reconciled with invoices and not paid unless correct.	
4 You should have a system to check goods are: (a) ordered (b) received (c) in satisfactory condition (d) that authority to pay is then given.	
5 Cheques should only be signed by properly authorized officials who will check the payment.	
6 A payment policy is need to cover: (a) discounts and whether to take them; (b) whether to pay before, on or after due dates.	If cash is not short taking discounts can be very beneficial.
7 If cash becomes short, you must decide on the policy to adopt. This includes which payments to delay and how to deal with the suppliers credit controllers.	

Credit Control of Purchases

Your credit control must not overlook the control of purchases. While poor credit assessment and poor debt collection are often major causes of cash shortages, it is the creditors who have not been paid who are likely to bring the business down.

The first step is to set maximum stock levels and re-order levels. This should avoid both excessive purchasing and running out of stock. The re-order levels need to keep stock at the minimum possible level consistent with not running out before the next delivery arrives. The levels cannot be agreed without some knowledge of the suppliers' ability to produce and deliver. There are a number of factors to consider when selecting suppliers which have a direct bearing on re-order levels. These are listed in Table 8.9.

Particular circumstances will often dominate the decisions about suppliers. For example, there may be only one supplier of a particular product and you will have to cope with his delivery problems. If there are a number of alternatives it is worth drawing up a table with the headings of Table 8.9 to compare the suppliers on the basis of all the factors.

Terms of credit are usually dictated by the practice ruling in an industry. However, negotiation of credit can be as important as negotiation of price. For example, it may be worth taking little or no credit if the price is low enough. However, it is likely initially that credit for your new business will be hard to get.

Over the longer term there is no doubt that the best way of creating and keeping supplier goodwill is to pay his bills on time. This may even ensure supply when shortages exist as the supplier is likely to treat good payers most favourably.

Finally, it is important to have a proper system to control outgoing payments. Some control points for such a system are also given in Table 8.9.

Surviving a Cash Crisis

Although it has already been said more than once no apology is made for repeating that businesses usually fail when cash runs out rather than because profit is not being made. Indeed, a fast-growing business can fail because its sales success is too great for its working capital facilities to cope. A cash crisis is, therefore, of the greatest significance to any business as it must be resolved or failure is likely.

One reason for urging you to use budgetary control and to monitor your progress conscientiously is to help you predict the possibility of a future cash crisis well before it occurs. This gives time to take corrective action. Also the ability to make the prediction and plan a way out makes it more likely that survival will be achieved. If a cash crisis occurs without warning, it is a sure sign of management's failure to manage properly. The chances of survival will

Table 8.10: Checklist for a Review of the Cash Needs of Your Business

FIXED ASSETS	*Notes*
Can premises be sold and leased back?	This takes time and cannot easily be arranged if your business is small and in financial difficulties.
Is there spare plant etc which can be sold?	In times of recession prices will not be good. Some finance may be secured on the assets and permission of the financier will be needed.
Review capital expenditure originally intended	If the sales are less than expected so should the needs for capital expenditure be.
Can replacements or new items be leased rather than purchased outright?	
Check the implications of all this possible action on your ability to raise or retain external finance.	

WORKING CAPITAL

Debtors

Consider ways to collect debts faster:

Can debtors be pressed for prompter payment?	Good credit control is needed with frequent chasing.
Can you alter your terms of business (e.g. some cash in advance)?	This will be resisted particularly if you are one of many suppliers of similar products.
Would offering discounts bring cash in faster?	This may be expensive compared with borrowing money but you may have no choice.
Can you improve the invoicing system, i.e. its speed and accuracy?	

Stocks

Review your stock. Can it be reduced?	There are likely to be some items where overstocking is greater than elsewhere. A fall in sales probably means you will become overstocked.
Will a reduction in buying be sufficient? Or should you sell off some stock in bulk?	A sale of stock at a loss can be worthwhile when cash is paramount.
Review re-order levels, i.e. the level at which re-ordering is done and the quantity bought.	Buying more frequently and in small quantities will tend to increase costs.
Is some stock not moving at all and should it be liquidated at any price?	A loss on cost is almost inevitable but cash will be generated.
Keep stock levels consistently monitored as the pattern and level of sales changes.	

Table 8.10 (*Cont'd.*)

Creditors

Do you pay sooner than you need?   It is common to pay later than the invoice specifies.

Do you take early payment discounts? If so perhaps you should change policy for the present?

Dividends

If you are paying them should you stop?   In a crisis the answer is likely to be yes.

Overhead Costs

Review all areas of cost.

Can some be dispensed with entirely?

Prepare detailed saving plans for each part of the business.

Can you buy more cheaply elsewhere?

Can you manage with less employees?   Redundancy costs must be allowed for.

Can you manage with less space and   This takes time.
sublet some?

Other Matters

Can you increase prices?   Small businesses are often too slow about this.

Are all sales lines profitable? If not should some be dropped as well as the associated overheads?

What ways of raising external finance are   If the business is in deep trouble there may
available?   be none.

---

also be low because of the lack of time for action.

Your new business is likely to be threatened at some point with cash crises because of delays in sales, production or some other vital factor. You must constantly look for the signs and proper, frequently reviewed, cash forecasting is the key tool. However, even mature businesses have cash crises due to complacency, the expectation of the continuation of the status quo or inadequate forecasting. This section briefly discusses some of the ways you can go about coping with an impending cash crisis provided you have seen it coming with enough time to take carefully thought out action.

A Review of the Cash Needs of the Business

Almost all aspects of any business have a cash implication. The first step is to undertake a thorough review of the position by looking at all the cash needs of the business and the ways of releasing cash or using less of it. Table 8.10 is a checklist of the major items to consider. This review will take time because of the need to examine in detail the various elements of your business, particularly costs.

An Action Plan

Your cost and cash review must include a careful cash forecast which may need several versions. These will reflect the various possible courses of action from the minor change of quicker debt collection to the major one of closing down part of the business.

The complete review must be discussed by the whole management who will need all the relevant information and the various courses of action before them. There are three main courses of action open to you if your business is not going to be able to survive within its present facilities without major surgery. These are:

1 Take management action, however unpleasant, to manage within cash resources. Despite a complete review, this either may not be possible or may not leave a viable business.
2 Raise outside finance. This will only be possible if you can demonstrate your ability to stem the cash losses and return the business to profitability. A proper plan and forecasts will help credibility.
3 If all else fails, sell the business before it does. This may not be easy if potential buyers see failure looming. They may take the view that they will buy more cheaply from a receiver.

There is no doubt that it is sometimes possible to survive difficult periods by just not paying creditors on time. Most companies 'stretch' their creditors a little from time to time and if you have serious difficulties you may have no choice. Unfortunately, some bills cannot be postponed. For example, the wage bill will never wait and if you cannot pay it without extra bank overdraft this may be the trigger which precipitates the appointment of a receiver by your bank.

The problems with paying creditors late are that it generates ill-will, it may involve withholding of vital supplies and it may result in writs. If cash is extremely tight the trick is to hold non-essential creditors at bay whilst paying enough to crucial suppliers who might withhold supplies and to creditors who might otherwise serve writs without caring about the consequences.

If a large backlog of creditors builds up it may be possible to reach agreement to pay these over an extended period of time, all creditors being likely to prefer small steady payments to nothing. Even the Inland Revenue can sometimes be persuaded to do a deal though all official bodies need to be treated with caution as they will not always be sympathetic to problems (whereas most trade suppliers will) and may not worry about losses on a wind-up. As a general rule it may be preferable to pay everybody something with explanations rather than leave some completely unpaid and risk writs.

Using delayed payment to creditors to survive cash crises can, therefore, certainly sometimes work. However, it involves a great deal of time being spent arguing with suppliers' credit controllers and may permanently damage your company's standing in the industry. You should not allow the need to arise merely from bad cash planning.

As mentioned above your action plan may involve raising money from outside. This type of emergency application is undoubtedly the most difficult type to prepare and the one with the least chance of success. Success depends on persuading the lender that the crisis can be overcome. Profit and cash flow forecasts are thus crucial as is assessment of your ability to overcome the crisis. It is important that credible explanations are provided of how the crisis occurred and why it will not recur. One reason your application may fail is that the financier considers that your company's management is deficient. However, increasingly investing institutions will consider applications from companies that will be viable provided additional finance and additional management support is available. This may involve you losing management control if the business is to be saved.

In summary, you will need to watch carefully for danger signs of impending cash crises. Constant review of future cash needs is required and early action is always desirable. If all of this is done your credibility if asking for outside finance will be helped. Finally, this is certainly a time to ask for help from your financial advisers and bankers. They will have the advantage of having seen it before and of being sufficiently detached that they may distinguish the wood from the trees more clearly than you can.

People

The importance of people to your new business is emphasized in Chapters 3, 8 and 9. Its success is more likely to depend on the right people than on any other single factor. It is therefore worth pulling together some of the points already made and expanding them in the context of the overall control of the business.

Controlling and managing people is probably the most difficult management skill because human beings are complex and not always predictable. While – if their jobs depend on it – you can force people to do as you say, this is not enough. You will need a happy, motivated group of employees if you want high productivity and loyalty. Good leadership, fair treatment and appropriate consultation are all essential ingredients of the man-management skills you will need to develop.

Recruiting and Training

The first essential is to make sure you recruit the right people. Bad recruitment of key staff could be a disaster and even the more humble members of staff are important in the early days.

Recruiting is a hazardous business even for large sophisticated companies which do it all the time. Occasional mistakes are unavoidable but need to be limited when your business is new and dependent on each member of staff. Unless you are skilled in this area you will probably be best advised to use personal recommendations where possible and seek professional help where not. This help might be from a good recruitment agency or, in the case of specific experts, from your professional advisers. A common mistake is to recruit a member of the family just because of the blood connection. This has frequently been a recipe for disaster if the choice is wrong and considerable bad feeling can be generated when you decide to part company.

Having recruited a new employee there is likely to be a need to train him. In the early days you will probably prefer to seek skilled people whose training will then only need to cover the ways in which you wish them to work. This may involve no more than close briefing followed by frequent supervision and monitoring for a trial period.

In due course you will have to organize training more formally for new recruits. Chapter 7 mentions the value of some official bodies who are concerned with training. You will also need to give thought to career development opportunities if you are to recruit and retain good people. This is stressed in Chapter 11 as an area of increasing importance to the growing business.

Organizing for Control

The earlier discussion of budgetary control emphasized the need to have a clear organizational structure and a proper delegation of authority to each manager. The structure should be published so that all employees are aware of who reports to each person. In each case this should give a brief description of the person's responsibilities and authority. It should cover who he reports to and who reports to him. If prepared properly, the job description will give the individual detailed guidance on what he can and cannot do and what he should and should not be doing.

A clear organizational structure backed up with job descriptions will be useful not only for budgetary control purposes but also for other monitoring of an employee's performance. He should expect to be judged on his performance of all of the elements of his job description.

Monitoring and Control

Good management of your business will need to include careful monitoring of employee performance. A first step is to agree targets of performance for all elements of each person's job description. Some of this will already have been done if you have adopted a full budgetary control system. However, some

142

targets may not directly relate to the budget and will need separate discussion. For example, the company secretary may be asked to review the available pension schemes and report to a board meeting in due course. At this stage, his actions have no direct connection with his responsibilities within the budgetary system.

The control of work output from your labour force is best done using a similar system to that already described for budgets. This involves:

1 Assessing what work load each individual or section already has.
2 Agreeing what performance standards are to be achieved.
3 Recording actual performance.
4 Comparing actual results with the standards set.
5 Taking appropriate action to control any departures of performance from agreed levels.

Obviously, supervision is an important part of this process. However, perhaps more important is the correct motivation of people to achieve the standards asked of them. This will involve good leadership, fair treatment and financial incentives.

If performance is persistently unsatisfactory you will need to involve disciplinary procedures. These are briefly discussed in Chapter 7, page 116.

9

Success or Failure?

General Comments

The majority of new businesses which are founded do not survive. Even skilled investing institutions who select propositions carefully expect to see a failure rate which may be around one in three. This underlines the risks which anybody takes who starts up his own business. However, the reduction in the average national failure rate from two-thirds or more to one-third or less, for those ventures backed by experienced investors, shows that there are some lessons which can be learned. This chapter summarizes the main ways in which the chances of success can be maximized and, conversely, the chances of failure reduced. Many of the points have been made elsewhere in the text but the topic is so important that drawing them together is worthwhile. Table 9.1 gives a checklist.

Four generalizations can be made which will be amplified later. Firstly, starting a new business involves taking risks. These cannot be avoided entirely but they can be minimized. As a general rule it is important to avoid tackling too many areas of new skills. Previous in-depth experience of the particular business sector is one of the best ways of achieving this. If you can couple this with selling to known customers, buying from known suppliers and employing known people then your business will have a much better than average chance of succeeding. However, if all of these are unknowns the chances of failure are very high.

Secondly, the most successful small businesses have some special feature which gives them an edge in the harsh competitive world. For example, this may be a unique or better product, a faster or more reliable service or a more personal service. What matters is that your new business should have a feature which appeals to customers when faced with the choice between various competing products. If this feature is strong it can command a premium price and the resulting high profit margin makes the financing of the business much easier. In hard times the special feature may ensure survival when others are struggling.

144

Table 9.1: Factors which affect Success and Failure

SUCCESS

People	Entrepreneurs	Flair, hardwork, dedicated and independent personalities. Previous relevant experience; avoid dramatic change. Good coverage of business skills required. Accounting experience.
	Recruited staff	Careful selection. Careful monitoring of performance. Motivation.
Business Plan		Careful preparation of all areas. Be conservative. Aim for special features of your product or service.
	Finance	Make sure enough is available.
	Profit margin	Try and keep high.
	Overheads	Avoid early and unnecessary overheads. Start business part-time if possible. Sub-contract where possible.
	Customers	Try and identify before beginning.
	Market	Assess carefully. Aim for a growing market or a clear gap.
	Location	This may be crucial to a retail business.
Controls		Have these right from the start. Simple but quick is better than sophisticated but slow.
Help from Others		Take professional advice. Use known contacts and develop others.

FAILURE

People	Make sure the partners are compatible. Have a defined basis for reaching decisions. In particular avoid 50:50 splits with no casting vote. Bad recruitment in the early days can be disastrous. Use others' expertise to recruit experts about whose skills you know little. Be careful when employing members of the family.
Business Plan	Avoid too little finance. Avoid high overheads. Have financial control from the start. Be careful about overdependence on one customer/supplier. Low profitability is dangerous. High gearing is dangerous. Mismatching is dangerous. In particular, too much short-term borrowing should be avoided.
Other Points	Avoid inflexibility. Avoid too rapid growth.

Thirdly, and perhaps most important, the people involved are crucial to the success of a new venture. Most professional investors agree that they would rather back good people with an indifferent idea than poor people with an outstanding idea. The reason is that the development of a new business is seldom smooth. There will be delays, crises, unexpected setbacks and changes in the business environment, none of which may be entirely foreseeable. Unless you have perseverance, dedication and the ability to adapt to changing circumstances your new business will probably not pull through the early formative years. It is ironic that a mature big business can probably survive better in normal economic circumstances with weak management than a new and small business. The reason is the frailty of the infant company with limited cash reserves, no loyal customers and no staff which can run the business despite management's failings. It is vital that the management of a new business has the ability and dedication to survive despite odds which will sometimes seem to be heavily stacked against them.

Finally, the importance of control must not be neglected. In the early days of your new business it will be easy to neglect proper controls because of other pressures. However, the ability to know where you now are in financial terms and where you are going is essential for survival. Early controls can be simple as it is more important that your control systems produce information quickly than that this information is fully detailed.

Increasing Your Chance of Success

People

The most important people are those who will run your new business. Not everybody is capable of making a success of a new, independent business. Even people with management experience as employees will find it tough being entirely on their own with no supporting organization on which to fall back. Inevitably, there will be problems and survival will sometimes depend more on a refusal to accept defeat than particular skills. Hard work, determination and guts will all be needed.

Apart from suitable personalities, your management will need a wide range of skills. These include management ability, selling, production, buying and accounting and will not always be well covered in a small group of entrepreneurs let alone by one man. Recognition of the obvious gaps and taking steps to fill them will help you ensure success. Accounting is a common gap and can be provided by good auditors.

Unless the business is to be very tiny you will need to recruit other people. Most people have limited experience of this and many businesses have failed because enough care has not been taken and mistakes have not been spotted until too late.

146

Business Plan

A large proportion of this book has been devoted to the planning that should precede the start of a new busines. The reason is that you cannot be too thorough in your preparation. Good plans, which are adhered to, enormously enhance the chances of success. Particular points which have already been made include:

Experience Try and build the business around your existing experience and skills as far as possible. This will greatly reduce the number of unknown areas with which you will have to cope.

Finance It is much safer to have too much money available than too little. Careful forecasting will be necessary to decide how much will be needed.

Margin A business which has a high level of profit on each sale is much more likely to succeed than one which does not. A high margin leaves more room for errors in calculating costs and usually means less outside finance will be required to run the business.

Overheads These should be kept as small as possible particularly before sales are generated. Until your business is profitable, overheads will eat into cash resources at an alarming rate and delays could then be disastrous.

Customers Your business will not succeed without good customers. If these are known before starting, the chances of success will greatly improve. A customer who knows and likes you and believes your product is good can be patient and helpful in the early stages.

Uniqueness The introduction to this chapter and Chapter 2 page 13 have mentioned the advantages of some special feature in the new business product or service.

Market This should be researched as carefully as possible. If it does not exist the business cannot survive. If it is large and growing, competition is not to be greatly feared.

Controls

Most good businesses are well controlled. This means the management always knows what is going on, can compare it with a plan of what should have been happening and can take action to correct problems. An important part of good control is prompt accurate feedback information.

Remember that weak financial control is the most common failing of small businesses. Indeed many big businesses fail for this reason.

A major problem for a new business can be that because there will seem to be so many things to do and too few people to do them, controls and information systems become neglected. They must have a place at the top of your list of priorities and not at the bottom. Most professional investors will insist on regular and frequent financial information and the imposition of this discipline is one of the ways an outside investor can help a business to succeed.

Help From Others

Good professional advice can be of great help in avoiding pitfalls which may endanger survival. Those who can help are bankers, accountants, lawyers and consultants.

One of the advantages of previous experience of the business area is that previous contacts can be used with success. Much of business life depends on knowing whom to approach to obtain a particular introduction or learn a particular piece of information. Good contacts are a valuable help to a new business and every effort should be made to develop them.

Avoiding Failure

We have discussed ways to increase your chances of success and, conversely, avoid failure. However, there are a number of specific pitfalls which have not yet been mentioned.

People

The most common cause of failure is simply bad management. Most businesses which have got into deep trouble and have survived have only done so because of a change of management. If you do not already have management skills you should recognize the need to develop these as a very high priority. Indeed, if you lack such skills your chances of failure through bad management can best be avoided by including an experienced manager in your team.

It is important to avoid a split in the management team. A common arrangement in a business which has two founders is a 50:50 share split and the sharing of the title 'Joint Managing Director'. This can be a recipe for disaster because there is no way to resolve disputes. Many businesses have failed because the management have spent more time fighting each other than the competition.

Bad recruitment of other staff can also be disastrous. It can be easiest to make this mistake when recruiting an expert from an area outside your experience. Recruitment of an accountant or bookkeeper is an example. One means of minimizing the chances of a recruiting error here is to use the advice of your financial adviser who should be able to do the technical interviewing for you.

Another common error is to recruit a family member who is chosen because of the family connection rather than his skill. Mistakes are often very hard to correct without a lot of bad feeling on both sides.

Business Plan

There are a number of common mistakes in business plans. The most common of all is not enough finance, particularly working capital. Because every business is likely to meet delays and setbacks, ample contingency is almost essential to avoid failure. Related to this is the need to keep costs to the minimum, especially before profits are made. You should remember that more businesses fail because of poor financial control (i.e. an inability to manage the affairs of the company within its financial resources) than for any other reason.

It is common advice to avoid overdependence on one customer or supplier. The reason for this is that you might be let down or, worse, deliberately squeezed until profitability disappears. However, a new business is usually short of orders in the early days. If, therefore, you can begin trading with a secure order from one big customer for all of your early sales you do not need to worry about income at a crucial stage. Indeed, sometimes the big customer will be helpful about payments and invoicing and general credit control is greatly simplified. A number of successful businesses have started this way but have then made sure they reduce the dependence as soon as possible. So, whilst overdependence on one customer (or supplier) is a reason for business failure it can be useful in the early days of the business.

Poor profitability is a common weakness. It may become poor in any business as the recent recessions have demonstrated. However, some entrepreneurs plan a business with a margin on sales (i.e. sales less direct costs) which is inadequate to cover overheads. Although it is commonly believed that owners of businesses are aiming to make money, it is not uncommon to see them aim for turnover growth at the expense of profits. If a business makes a large percentage of profit on its sales it is easier to plan and to finance the business.

Finally, your business plan should allow for a proper matching of finance to its use as mentioned in Chapter 5. Also, too much borrowed money compared with the share capital can be dangerous. This ratio is called gearing. The danger of high gearing is that the interest paid in servicing borrowings becomes a high percentage of the profit before interest. This means that profit may not have to fall much before losses after interest are made. Increasing interest rates may then be sufficient to produce losses. In other words the profitability of the business may be more dependent on outside circumstances than is wise.

Other Matters

It is important to avoid inflexibility. Your business must survive in a world which will often be changing outside your control. You must therefore be prepared to make changes and not to stick rigidly to plans which circumstances have made impractical. Because change will usually happen gradually, good information systems will be needed to spot it. Regular meetings and good management decisions will then be needed to alter the course of the business to cope with the observed changes. This all sounds rather frightening and indeed it can be. However, small businesses are often much better at adapting to change than large businesses which have considerable momentum in a fixed direction. An analogy is the ability of a sailing dinghy to change course in an emergency compared with an oil tanker.

Ironically, a business can fail from apparently being very successful. Rapid growth is dangerous for several reasons. First, increased turnover usually means that increased working capital is required because of an increase in stock and debtors. Many businesses do not generate profit fast enough to finance rapid increases in turnover. It follows then that unless adequate borrowing facilities are available, the business will be in trouble despite its success in selling. Other problems also follow with rapid growth. The organization, its management, staff and control systems usually cannot keep pace. It is vital to consolidate growth from time to time to check that the business is in a sound shape before moving forward. Even large businesses have these problems despite management with years of experience, so the small business needs to treat very rapid growth with extreme caution.

Summary

There are many reasons for success or failure. Many of these are well-known and experience shows that there are a number of features a new business should aim for which can maximize its chances of survival. Conversely, there are a number of well established warning signs if failure is to be avoided. If you plan properly with these features, good and bad, borne carefully in mind you will certainly be in a position to avoid the worst mistakes. Finally, however, the success of your business will depend on its people. They must have faith in themselves and have the tenacity and sheer stubborness to survive difficulties. Survival will involve risks however carefully you have planned. But if you think you might fail (as opposed to recognizing the dangers and planning to avoid or minimize them) you are not likely to succeed if the going gets difficult. Unless you have faith in your ability to succeed you should probably not try.

10
Outside Help

Introduction

No businessman is an expert in every professional discipline which he may need. Most experienced businessmen recognize this and, in general, the more mature a business is the more it turns to outside professional advice when appropriate. Ironically the new businessman, who is most in need of help, often is the least likely to seek it. He may argue it is too expensive or that he does not know anybody good to turn to.

Most outside assistance is not free and often the better the quality of the adviser the higher the cost. However, cheapness can be false economy as many people who have had cheap tax advice can confirm. Indeed, poor professional advice can be worse than none at all and you should aim for good rather than cheap advice. This poses the problem of where to find good advice. Unfortunately, professional qualifications are no guarantee. There is no doubt the choice is best made with the benefit of personal recommendations from others who have used the adviser and found him to be good. If, after employing an adviser, you are not satisfied with the service you receive do not hesitate to make a change. It is a common mistake to complain about a service but not to do anything about it.

This chapter discusses the main categories of professionals who can offer advice. Besides them there are some other bodies such as government departments which can be of valuable assistance for certain purposes including the provision of finance. These too are discussed.

Contacts

Contacts can be useful in all aspects of business life. They can introduce customers, recommend suppliers, help locate premises and help in many other important ways. Even something trivial like a faulty telephone switchboard will often be repaired quicker if you know the repair man or his supervisor personally. In addition, contacts can recommend good professional advisers from their own experience of them. They should, therefore, be cultivated from the outset. They may include friends in the same industry, senior employees of customers, suppliers and others with whom your business will deal. Because of their value, it is worth making deliberate attempts to make new contacts and, perhaps, join the clubs where local businessmen meet.

Accountants

Most accountants whom you might approach for help will be employed by, or be partners in, a firm of chartered accountants (or, less commonly, certified accountants). All limited companies must have their accounts audited annually by independent accountants and this means that much of the work of any firm of accountants is audit work. An accountant may be the most important outside adviser that you will employ because of the vital services he can supply. These include:

1 Auditing.
2 General financial advice. This can include help with your business plan especially the cash and profit forecasts.
3 Tax advice. Even the largest business tends to seek some tax advice from outside and a good tax adviser can save far more money than his fees. However, a bad adviser can be disastrous.
4 Information on overseas opportunities. This includes legal requirements, tax and local contacts.
5 Specific consultancy and other special project work. This may include the design of financial control systems.
6 Help with routine accountancy. In the early days your business is unlikely to be able to justify the employment of a full-time accountant and may have to manage with a part-time bookkeeper. In such cases, the auditors can prepare, say, monthly accounts to help with early management control.
7 Help with recruitment of accounting staff. The auditors are more likely than you to know what to look for in either a bookkeeper or a qualified accountant.

You will now realize that the choice of auditor is a vital one. It makes sense to be very careful and, preferably, use personal recommendation. If you are approaching a source of outside finance it may be able to recommend good auditors. Indeed, it is likely to insist that acceptable auditors are employed.

If you cannot make a choice from personal recommendations there are some rules of thumb. First, it is always tempting to use a local, one man firm because it is cheap. However, no one man firm can supply the range of services which your business might require. In addition some subjects, such as tax, are so technical that all firms of accountants except the very smallest have experts who specialize in it. This means the tax advice available is better than any general practitioner can supply. At the other end of the scale the largest firms may not always be able to offer the personal service that you want. For these reasons a medium-sized firm might be the best choice, although the large firms have recently made real improvements in their ability to provide a good service to the small company.

Banks and Investing Institutions

A bank manager is an obvious person to turn to for advice on financial matters. A good bank manager can be invaluable not only for advice but also for introductions to accountants, solicitors and other professionals. However, each of the major UK clearing banks has several thousand managers and it is not reasonable to expect each of them to be skilled in corporate matters – no big employer can claim to have three thousand or more talented employees! So, even a bank manager needs to be chosen with care and preferably by personal recommendation.

A useful rule of thumb is that the small local branch at which you have your personal account is not likely to be the best place to go for good advice on corporate matters or for imaginative corporate lending. Increasingly, the big banks are organizing themselves to have teams of corporate specialists either in big branches or special offices.

A good bank manager is a valuable ally who will sometimes help you beyond the normal calls of duty. If you have a recommendation to a manager such as this you should take it. Like all other professionals, the very good ones are few and far between despite the standard to which the profession aspires.

Similarly, if you approach a financial institution for support you may find that much more than finance is available. Sometimes the institution may wish to appoint a director to your board. If he is good this can be an excellent feature of their investment. However, if he is not it is merely a financial burden and inconvenience. An investing institution should also be a good source of introductions to accountants, solicitors and perhaps its other customers.

A particular strength of a good investing institution is the confidence that you should get from knowing that your business plan has stood up to detailed scrutiny by professional investors. If a good institution invests, you can also be reasonably sure your gearing and asset financing are properly structured. The institution will also probably force you to prepare proper management accounts on a regular basis which is a valuable discipline.

Solicitors

All businesses need a solicitor to handle formal registration and other corporate legal matters. However, solicitors can offer more than this. Like

153

accountants, they can be a useful source of financial advice and contacts. Many are also able to offer specialist advice on tax and corporate structure.

The commonest mistake you might make is to use the solicitor who conveyanced the purchase of your house. The chances are that he is not a specialist in corporate matters though, if you are lucky, his firm will have experts to whom you will be referred. You should recognize that solicitors, like accountants, are often specialists and you will need a good corporate lawyer not a conveyancing, divorce or criminal specialist. Again, recommendation from someone you trust is the best route to a good solicitor and cheapness is not something you should seek at the expense of quality.

Official Bodies

There are a number of official bodies which can be of great help to you. One starting point is your local Small Firms Information Centre as a useful source of ideas and help. Do recognize that such offices cannot hope to be real experts in commercial matters. However, they offer free and impartial advice. Other useful addresses are given in Appendix 2.

There are a number of areas of help which might be available from government bodies. These include:

1 A regional development grant towards the cost of your buildings and plant if you intend to manufacture in an assisted area.
2 Assistance with converting premises, or the provision of government-owned factory at a favourable rent (possibly with the first two years rent free).
3 A grant if you are in an industry creating jobs in assisted areas or one to which specific aid is being given.
4 Loan or other finance through one of the government organizations

One of the most appealing forms of government aid is subsidized money or grants. As this aid is frequently changing, details of current schemes are not felt worth listing here. Instead, your local Small Firms Information Centre will be able to give you up to date details. However, the principles of current aid are not so likely to change and can be summarized as follows:

1 Most subsidized money and other aid is directed at depressed areas whose definition changes from time to time. This aid includes grants and assistance with premises and rent relief.
2 Some subsidized money and grants are industry specific. These are usually industries which the government wishes to support or stimulate and the Department of Industry can always give details.
3 Some subsidized money is available to those who offer jobs to people made redundant by a troubled industry. An example is the finance from the European Coal and Steel Community (ECSC). This is for companies making

capital investment and who are prepared to offer jobs to redundant steel or coal industry employees in priority to others.

4 Small and new companies have been a priority in recent years as politicians have recognized the importance of them to the health of the economy. Specific support schemes have therefore been introduced in this area. Recent examples include (i) a government loan scheme where the government guarantees to an approved financial organization that it will carry 80% of the financial risk in return for a fee paid by the customer and (ii) a tax incentive scheme to motivate individuals to invest their money in new, private businesses which are not run by themselves. The scheme allows the individual to claim tax relief on the money he invests.

Consultants

Many people believe consultants to be expensive and of dubious value. However, used properly they can be a valuable help. Particular uses might be to install a computer system to control accounting information, to advise management on the structure of a growing company, or to help recruit new staff. All of these specific projects may be difficult for you because of shortage of time, inadequate experience or the need to have an objective outside view.

There are a number of firms of consultants who will do project work for the small company. Some of these are attached to large accounting firms, some are part of other financial groups and some are independent. They deserve consideration when a project is beyond the immediate means of your company's management.

Others

There are a host of other professionals from whom you can get expert advice in a particular area of knowledge. As with the other groups, personal recommendation is the best way of finding good advice. Otherwise choose carefully and if you do not like the advice do not take it. These professionals include:

1 Estate agents to help with finding premises.
2 Insurance brokers to help with insurance which is a complex matter for a corporate body. It will include pension schemes.
3 Recruiting agencies which can be a valuable help with staff recruiting. Usually they will advertise and do preliminary interviews, offering you a short list from which to choose.
4 Temporary employment bureaux. The classic example is temporary secretarial work but other skills can be bought on a short-term basis. This may be of particular value to you at holiday time or if your requirement for labour fluctuates considerably.

11

Getting Bigger

Introduction

Many businesses begin very small and are controlled by just one man. Often he runs the business by the seat of his pants and has no close confidants or critics to whom he turns for advice. The business then grows using the same formula. Unfortunately, there are problems with this approach which are often realized too late so that the transition to a more professionally managed and controlled business is a painful one.

This chapter briefly considers some of the problems which occur as businesses grow and mentions some of the solutions. In all cases the best approach is to anticipate the problems and take action to avoid them before they occur. Indeed, this has been a recurrent theme throughout the book. The Reading List gives some suggestions for further information on this important topic.

Planning and Control

As your business grows you will need to adapt its management style, organizational structure and control systems. Careful planning for the future is an essential prerequisite of this. Thus the first thing your growing company needs to do is plan. This may expose a lack of proper objectives which will need to be agreed before plans can be drawn up. This approach was first recommended in Chapter 3 when discussing the initial business plan but it is one which is not commonly adopted by small companies. If you learn to plan from the outset your company will be prepared for growth. If you do not, not only will the need to plan become stronger and stronger as your business grows but also the adoption of a plan may become more difficult.

The emphasis of planning for a small company is likely to be short-term (one or two years at most) rather than the rolling five or ten year long-term plans which are often prepared by large companies. Long-term planning is essential for large companies because they are subject to influences from changes in markets, economics and politics which they cannot ignore. In addition, their very size means they have considerable inertia which makes change slow. Most of this does not apply to the small company and long-term planning is of more doubtful value for it. However, the value of short-term planning is considerable as we have already discussed in Chapter 8.

Planning on its own is useless without the ability to monitor and control progress against the plan. This was mentioned in Chapter 8 as the key step towards budgetary control. This is a technique which must certainly be adopted by your company at some stage of its growth and sooner is better than later. As your company grows its control systems will have to be progressively better as you will gradually and inevitably lose a detailed feel for the performance of every aspect of the business.

Planning will also point towards the need for changes in your company, its structure and working methods. These will take time to implement as acceptance of new ideas must be obtained from all your key staff. This emphasizes a point made in Chapter 9 that problems can occur if growth is too rapid and allows too little time for the organization to adapt. Hence the advice to consolidate from time to time and check that all is running smoothly and is ready for the next growth phase before it starts.

Delegation and an Organization

It was mentioned in Chapter 8 that budgetary control needs authority for each budgetary item to be assigned to one individual. He will then be responsible for its control. More generally, it is obvious that as your business grows one man cannot have a detailed knowledge and control of all its elements. Apart from there being too few hours in the day, no one man will have all the professional skills that will be required. So in delegating authority you will not just make subordinates responsible for things you do not have time to do but, in some cases, they will do their job better than you could.

Some people find the transition from a one-man business to a professionally-managed organization a difficult one if they have built the business from scratch. Indeed, it is hardest of all to plan and organize the management such that you can eventually be dispensed with. A common mistake in smaller, mature companies is that the ageing managing director does not even have a suitable candidate to replace him on retirement.

To develop your management organization you need a properly published organization chart and job descriptions of those on the chart. The organization chart must show who is responsible to, and reports to, whom. The job description will need to list exactly what the person's responsibilities are and how far his authority extends. Only then is it possible for efficient decision-making to take place with each person knowing what he can and cannot do and to whom he is answerable for his actions. As your organization grows there will be a need from time to time to recruit a new professional as the requirement for a particular skill becomes great enough to justify a specialist. Skills which may not originally be affordable, or necessary, full-time are accounting, marketing, development engineering and personnel management. Of all of these, the one which is most often neglected and with possible dire consequences is accounting.

A good qualified accountant brings with him the skills to help set up the budgetary control and management information systems and keep them up to date. He should also be able to implement the computerization of the company's financial information and run credit control and other vital functions. This is a far greater contribution than just keeping the books.

Finally, as your company grows so will its personnel needs. Means for recruiting, training and developing careers of staff will need to be found. This is often a problem for the smaller company as the justification for a full-time qualified personnel manager usually occurs at a relatively late stage of growth. Until a personnel manager can be justified, someone else will have to do the job although ad hoc assignments can be carried out by consultants. Often the accountant who controls cash and wage payments anyway can take on the day-to-day responsibilities of a personnel manager.

People

The importance of having the right people involved in your company if it is to be successful has been discussed in Chapters 3, 8 and 9. One advantage of growth is that the business should become less dependent on a very few key people.

As your business grows it will need to give increasing importance to personnel management. Any larger business needs to have proper training facilities and career development policies for its staff. Once the business is managed by several people there will be ample scope for staff to learn management by first supervising others and then taking increasing management responsibilities. This is not only important if your business is to be properly run and organized but is vital if good ambitious people are to be recruited and retained.

As your business grows, you will probably also find an increasing need to formalize certain aspects of the way people are managed. This will include salary scales and their formal review, reviews of staff performance for promotion, unified policies on holidays, sickness and many other things. The time will come when you will need to consider employing a professional personnel manager in order to cope with all this. Despite the importance of people to most businesses this is often the last professional skill which is recruited as few smaller businesses feel they can justify the cost.

The hardest thing for many entrepreneurs to accept is that they should eventually make plans for their replacement on retirement. It is sad that many excellent smaller companies have no obvious candidate to replace the managing director who often stays in the job until he is really no longer the force that he once was. You should come to terms with training someone to replace you and your partners in due course and try and avoid leaving it too late. This is also an important element in the career development prospects for the younger managers and a feeling that the top jobs will not be available may cause good people to leave for opportunities elsewhere.

Outside Finance

As your business grows it may, perhaps for the first time, have a need for outside finance. This will emerge naturally from the planning process but the consequences will need to be carefully considered. As mentioned in Chapter 5, outside finance may involve some restrictions on the activities of your business unless prior consultation with financiers is made. It may also involve a dilution of your and your partners' equity stakes. This relates back to your personal objectives. For example, do you want 100% of the shares at all costs? Or do you want that fastest possible growth provided you can keep at least 51% of the shares (and legal control of the business)? These issues will need periodical review as your business grows and new opportunities occur which can only be financed by some use of outside facilities.

The key to raising outside finance is, of course, properly prepared plans. This is no different to raising finance for a new business but will tend to be easier as the business establishes a track record which lends credibility to its management skills, plans and forecasts.

Appendix 1
Technical Terms

AGED DEBTORS (OR CREDITORS)
Debtors are arranged in date order and grouped by say, months.
This is particularly useful to check the trends in debtor payments.

ARTICLES OF ASSOCIATION
A legal requirement of a limited company which lays out the rules
by which the company is to be managed.

AUDITED ACCOUNTS
Accounts of a company which are verified by an independent
accountant. They are an annual legal requirement for a limited
company.

AUDITOR
A qualified accountant who independently verifies the accounts
of a company.

BREAKEVEN
To be making neither a profit nor a loss. Breakeven turnover is
often calculated to indicate the turnover above which profit will
be made.

BALANCE SHEET
A statement at a particular time of all the assets and liabilities of a
business. The assets must equal the liabilities, hence the name.

BUDGET
A plan of what should be achieved by the company during the
coming period which is broken down into sections and agreed
with each manager responsible for its achievement.

BUDGETARY CONTROL
The control of a business by use of budgets. The actual performance during each period must be compared with budget to

identify departures from budget. Corrective action can then be taken.

BUSINESS NAME
The trading name of a business if it is different to the names of all the partners (for a partnership) or the incorporated name (for a limited company).

BUSINESS PLAN
A complete plan for a new business or venture including financial forecasts.

CALL
A loan is at call if it is repayable on demand (i.e. without an agreed period of notice). A bank overdraft is call money.

CAPITAL EXPENDITURE
Money spent on the purchase of fixed assets.

CASH FLOW
The passage of money through a business. A cash flow forecast is an estimate of the money to be received and the money to be paid during a future period. It shows how the cash balance is likely to increase or decrease as time goes by.

CONTINGENCY
An allowance for overspending (or underestimates) in preparing a forecast of financial needs. It is also used when preparing accounts to mean an allowance for liabilities that might be incurred.

CONTRACT OF EMPLOYMENT
The rules governing the employment of an individual of which his employer must give him a copy by law.

CONTRIBUTION
See Gross Profit.

CONVERTIBLE LOAN
A loan, some or all of which may be converted into ordinary shares in the business. Conversion is usually at the lender's option.

CORPORATE OBJECTIVES
A statement of the fundamental aims of the business expressed in specific rather than vague terms.

COSTING
The analysis of the total cost of a product.

CREDIT
The giving of a period of grace to a buyer before he must pay for goods already received.

CREDIT CONTROL
The control of the credit given to others by a business. It includes the control of debt collection.

CREDIT FACTORING
A form of short-term finance where the lender makes advances against sales invoices and then collects those debts to repay the loan.

CREDIT INSURANCE
Insurance of the outstanding debts of a business against risks of non-payment.

CREDIT RISK
The risk that a debt will not be paid if credit is allowed. It usually refers to the risk that the creditor will go bankrupt.

CREDITOR
He who owes money to a business. Trade creditors are usually the supplier of raw materials or other goods.

CURRENT ASSETS
Amounts owed to the business and other items which will be converted into cash within 12 months. The main items are usually debtors, stock and cash.

CURRENT LIABILITIES
Amounts owed by the business and due within 12 months. The main items are usually creditors and the bank overdraft.

DEBENTURE
A form of security given to a lender over some or all of the assets of a business. This restricts the ability of others to take security and means that if the business fails the unsecured (including trade) creditors will only see their money back after the secured creditor (the debenture holder) is paid in full.

DEBTOR
He who owes money to the business. In any business using sales invoices the customers become debtors.

DEFERRED TAX
An accounting provision usually arising from the difference between accounting and tax treatments of depreciation.

DEPRECIATION
An accounting treatment to allow for the fixed assets consumed in the course of trading.

DISCOUNTS
Usually encountered as (1) a percentage reduction in the invoiced amount for early settlement or (2) a percentage reduction in the cost per unit for bulk buying.

DIVIDENDS
Payments to shareholders from the profits of the business. They are usually declared as x pence per ordinary share. There is a tax credit to the shareholder and a tax charge to the business at the time of the payment.

ECGD
Export Credit Guarantee Department – a Government Department which provides various forms of credit insurance to cover the risks involved with exports.

EMPLOYERS LIABILITY INSURANCE
A legal requirement for all employers to insure their employees against injury or accident at work.

ENTREPRENEUR
A person who takes commercial risks to try and make a profit.

EQUITY
Any type of shares in a company which will share in the profits and capital value of the business without limit. Ordinary shares are the simplest example.

FINANCIAL CONTROL
The control of all aspects of the financial affairs of a business.

FIXED ASSETS
Permanent assets held by a business for more than one year for the purpose of earning profit. Buildings, plant and equipment are examples.

FIXED COSTS
Costs of running a business which do not vary with the level of sales (or production).

FORECAST
A prediction of the performance of a business over a future period. The common ones are profit and cash flow forecasts.

GEARING
A measure of the relative level of borrowings of a company. It is often (but not always) defined as total borrowings including bank overdraft divided by shareholders' funds (or capital accounts for a partnership).

GROSS PROFIT
The profit on each sale (often expressed as a percentage of turnover) after deduction of all costs which relate directly to that sale. This is also called contribution.

HIRE PURCHASE
A form of equipment financing where the lender hires the asset to the borrower for an agreed period. At the end of the financing period the borrower can exercise an option at a nominal price to buy the asset.

INCORPORATION
The process of registering a company with limited liability for the shareholders.

INSOLVENT
It usually means the failure of a business to pay its debts as they fall due. It can also be used to mean the business has more liabilities than assets (due to losses).

LEASING
A form of equipment financing where the asset never passes into the legal ownership of the business. Instead it is rented to it for an indefinite period.

LIMITED COMPANY
A company whose shareholders have their liability for the debts of the business limited to the amount (if any) unpaid on their shares. A company can also be limited by guarantee. Here the owners provide a limited guarantee which would be called upon if the business failed.

LIMITED LIABILITY
The concept behind limited companies and limited partnerships where, provided proper registration is made, the owners of a business can avoid liability for all the debts of a business venture. Their liability is limited to any amounts unpaid on their shares.

LONG-TERM FINANCE
Usually any loan repayable over seven years or more is considered long-term. Shares, being usually not repayable, are also long-term finance.

MANAGEMENT ACCOUNTS
Profit and loss statements for a business for a particular period for use by the management in monitoring and controlling performance.

MATCHING
The financing of assets required by a business over a period appropriate to the life of the asset.

MEDIUM-TERM FINANCE
Any form of finance repayable over 3 to 7 years. Hire purchase and leasing are usually in this category.

MEMORANDUM OF ASSOCIATION
This is a legal requirement for a limited company. It is a kind of charter setting out the activities of the company. See also Articles of Association which always accompany the Memorandum.

NATIONAL HEALTH INSURANCE
A legal requirement for all employers (whose employees must also make required contributions) which covers payments to the National Health Service. Self employed people must also pay. Payments to the State Pension Scheme are also deducted through the same mechanism.

NET PROFIT
Usually profit after deduction of all overheads including finance charges but before charging tax.

ORDINARY SHARES
Shares in a company which are entitled to all of the capital growth of the business and which can receive dividends up to the limit of profits made.

OVERDRAFT
The agreement by a bank which allows an account holder to draw from a current account amounts to an agreed limit beyond a zero cash balance. This finance is usually at call i.e. repayment can be demanded without notice.

OVERHEADS
Those costs of running a business which do not directly relate to making goods or making sales. They include finance costs, rent and rates.

PROFIT MARGIN
This can be gross or net. Gross margin is the percentage profit which is present in each sale after deduction of costs directly

related to the sale. Net profit margin is the percentage profit after deducting all costs except tax. Both are measures of the profitability of the business.

PARTNERSHIP
A group of people carrying on a business together with the intention of making a profit.

PERSONAL GUARANTEE
This usually means individuals agree to become liable for the bank overdraft of their business should the business fail. A guarantee may be limited in amount or unlimited.

PHASED FORECASTS
A forecast which is written with more than one version depending on different levels of sales.

PREFERENCE SHARES
Shares which are paid out at a fixed amount in preference to ordinary shares on a liquidation or sale. Dividends are usually fixed and again are paid in preference to any ordinary dividend.

PRIMARY PERIOD
The period when a finance company receives the return of its cost and profit from a leasing transaction.

RECEIVER
A person appointed by a secured lender (under the terms of the security given by his debenture) to sell the assets of the business as he thinks fit in an attempt to recover the debt. This power usually becomes operative if a business fails to pay interest or capital of a loan on time.

ROLLING FORECASTS
A forecast (profit or cash flow) which is always kept up to date. For example, every 3 months the forecast is revised to cover the coming 12 months.

SECONDARY PERIOD
The period in a finance lease after the lender has recovered his cost and profit. The rental is then usually nominal but keeps the ownership of the asset with the financier which is necessary for tax purposes.

SENSITIVITY
The extent to which a forecast will vary if a certain item in the forecast is wrong. For example, the sensitivity of profit to a 10% shortfall in forecast sales.

SHAREHOLDERS FUNDS
The total share capital and retained profits of a company.

SHORT-TERM FINANCE
Any finance repayable within a 3 year period. This includes overdrafts.

SOLE TRADER
A person who enters into business without partners and without registering as a limited company.

TAX ALLOWANCE
An amount which may be deducted by an individual or company from his taxable income in calculating his liability for tax.

TAX AVOIDANCE
The legal planning of tax affairs to minimize the amount of tax payable.

TAX EVASION
The illegal planning of tax affairs to reduce a tax bill. Falsification of profits is an example.

TAX RELIEF
An amount which, in certain circumstances, may reduce an individual's, or company's, tax liability.

TAXABLE PROFIT
The profit on which tax must be paid. This is calculated by adjusting the accounting profit according to tax rules.

VARIABLE COSTS
A cost which varies with the level of sales.

VARIANCE
The difference between a budgeted figure and the actual figure achieved. A positive variance is better than budget, a negative variance is worse than budget.

WRIT
A legal instrument, issued by the court, obliging a debtor to make payment or face liquidation.

Appendix 2

Sources of Help

Area of Need	*Help With*	*Contact*

ACCOUNTING	Audit
	Management
	  information systems
	Professional advice
	Forecasting
	Tax planning
		The Accountants Institutes
		  publish lists of members
		  and addresses:
		
		Institute of Chartered
		  Accountants in England
		  and Wales
		PO Box 433
		Chartered Accountants Hall
		Moorgate Place
		London EC2P 2BJ
		(01 628 7060)
		
		Institute of Chartered
		  Accountants in Ireland
		7 Fitzgibbon Place
		Dublin 2
		Eire
		(0001 76041)
		
		Institute of Chartered
		  Accountants in Scotland
		27 Queen Street,
		Edinburgh EH2 1GA
		(031 225 5673)

		Association of Certified Accountants 20 Lincoln's Inn Fields, London WC2A 3EE (01 242 6855)
CREDIT CONTROL	Credit Checks	Dun & Bradstreet 26 Clifton Street London EC2 (01 247 4377)
		United Association for the Protection of Trade Ltd 145 London Road Croydon (01 680 7400)
	Insurance	Credit and Guarantee Insurance Co Ltd Colonial House, Mincing Lane London EC3R 7PN (01 626 5846)
		Trade Indemnity PLC Trade Indemnity House 12–34 Great Eastern Street London ECA 3AX (01 739 4311)
COMPANY COMPARISONS	Statistical Performance Comparisons	Centre for Interfirm Comparison 25 Bloomsbury Square London WC1A 2PJ (01 637 8406)
		8 West Stockwell St Colchester Essex CO1 1HN (0206 62274)
EMPLOYING PEOPLE	Recruiting Training	Job Centres of the Department of Employment Employment agencies Training Services Division Manpower Services

		Commission 162 Regent Street London W1 (01 214 6000)
	PAYE etc	Local tax office brochure P7 gives details
	General Advice	Selkirk House High Holborn London WC1 (01 836 1213) Local Jobcentre/ employment office See organizations listed under GENERAL ADVICE Manpower Services Commission
	Industrial Problems	Advisory, Conciliation and Arbitration Service (ACAS) Head Office 11–12 St James's Square London SW1Y 4LR (01 214 6000)
EXPORTING	Credit Risks	ECGD Publicity Branch Aldermanbury House Aldermanbury London EC2P 2EC (01 606 6699 X 695)
	General Information/ help and advice	British Overseas Trade Board Export Services and Promotion Division Export House Ludgate Hill London EC4M 7HU (01 248 5757) or export section of the nearest Department of Industry regional office

	Exports	British Export Houses Association 69 Cannon Street London EC4N 5AB (01 248 4444)
		Central Office of Information Hercules Road London SE1 7DU (01 928 2345 ext 214)
	Technical Help with Exports	Technical Help to Exporters British Standards Institution Marylands Avenue Hemel Hempstead Herts, HP2 4SQ. (0442 3111)
		British Overseas Trade Board Offices 1 Victoria Street London SW1H OET (01 215 7877)
FACTORY/PREMISES REGULATIONS	Fire	Local fire advisory centre
	Health and Safety	Health and Safety Executive of your local Department of Health and Social Security
	Planning Permission	Planning department of the Local Council
	Advertising Signs	Local Authority Planning Department
	Building Regulations	Local Authority Planning Department
	Local Bye-law Regulations	Local Authority Planning Department
	Licences For Restaurants etc	Local Authority Planning Department
	Factories Act	Health and Safety Executive

	Offices Shop and Railway Premises Act	Local Authority Environmental Health Department
FRANCHISING	General Advice	British Franchise Association Limited 15 The Poynings Iver Bucks SLO 9DS (0753 653546)
GENERAL ADVICE	Accountants (see ACCOUNTING) Counselling Information Brochures	Many big firms produce helpful brochures Small Firms Service Department of Industry Small Firms Centre (Dial 100 and ask for Freefone 2444) or Small Firms Division Department of Industry Abell House John Islip Street London SW1 4LN (01 211 3000) In Scotland the service is provided by: Scottish Development Agency 120 Bothwell Street Glasgow G2 7JP (041 248 2700) In Wales the Welsh office provides an information service: Industry Department Government Buildings Babalfa Cardiff CF4 6AT (0222 62131) In Northern Ireland an information service is provided by the Department of Commerce:

		Chichester House 64 Chichester Street Belfast BT1 4JX (0232 34488)
INSURANCE	National Insurance	Local office of Department of Health and Social Security
	General Insurances	British Insurance Brokers' Association Fountain House 130 Fenchurch Street London EC3M 5DJ (01 623 9043)
		Corporation of Mortgage Finance and Life Assurance Brokers Ltd 88 Victoria Road Aldershot Hampshire (0252 315681)
		Insurance Brokers Registration Council 15 St Helens Place London EC3A 6DS (01 588 4387)
LEGAL MATTERS	Forming a company General legal advice	Qualified solicitors are listed by: The Law Society 113 Chancery Lane London WC2 (01 242 1222)
	Registration of a Company	The Companies Registration Office Crown Way Maindy Cardiff CF4 3U2 (0222 388588)
	Registration of a Company for Scotland	The Companies Registration Office 102 George Street

Edinburgh 2
(031 225 5774)

MARKETING	Help with market studies General advice	British Marketing Research Bureau Ltd Saunders House 53 The Mall London W5 (01 567 3060)

Institute of Sales and
    Marketing Management
Concorde House
24 Warwick New Road
Royal Leamington Spa
CU32 5JH
(0926 37621)

Institute of Public Relations
1 Great James Street
London WC1
(01 405 5505)

Institute of Marketing
Moor Hall
Cookham
Berkshire SL6 9QH
(06285 24922)

The British Direct Mail
    Marketing Association
New Burlington Street
London W1
(01 437 4485

The Industrial Market
    Research Society
Bird Street
Lichfield
Staffordshire

The Market Research
    Society
15 Belgrave Square
London W1X 8PF
(01 235 4709)

PATENTS	Registration details, advice etc	Patent Advice and Service Bureau 7 Store Buildings Lincoln's Inn London WC2 (01 242 2535)
		Chartered Institute of Patent Agents Staple Inn Buildings London WC1 (01 405 9450)
		Department of Trade Patent Office 25 Southampton Buildings London WC2A 1AY (01 405 8721)
PROPERTY PURCHASE	Finding premises	Local estate agents New Town Development Corporation Local authorities Local Small Firms Centre (dial 100 and ask for Freefone 2444)
		English Industrial Estates Corporation Team Valley Gateshead Tyne and Wear NEL1 ONA (0632 876071)
		COSIRA 141 Castle Street Salisbury SP1 3TP (0722 6255)
PUBLIC SECTOR ASSISTANCE	General advice	Small Firms Centres (*see* GENERAL ADVICE)
TAX ADVICE		Local tax office Any qualified accountant
OTHER USEFUL ADDRESSES		British Institute of Management Small Business Information Service

Management House
Parker Street
London WC2B 5PT
(01 405 3456)

Local chamber of
    commerce
Address from:
Association of British
    Chamber of Commerce
Sovereign House
212A Shaftesbury Avenue
London WC2H 8EW
(01 240 5831)

Council for Small Industries
    in Rural Areas (COSIRA)
141 Castle Street
Salisbury
Wiltshire SP1 3TP
(0722 6255)

Welsh Development
    Agency
Treforest Industrial Estate
Pontypridd
Mid Glamorgan CF37 5UT
(044 385 2666)

Northern Ireland
    Development Agency
100 Belfast Road
Holywood
County Down BT1 9QX
(023 17 4232)

Scottish Development
    Agency
120 Bothwell Street
Glasgow G2 7JP
(041 248 2700)

National Federation of Self
    Employed and Small
    Businesses Ltd
32 St Annes Road West
Lytham St Annes

Lancs FY8 1NY
(0253 720911)

Institution of Management
   Consultants
23 Cromwell Place
London SW7 2LG
(01 584 7285)

Association of Independent
   Businesses
The Lettering Centre
Trowbray House
108 Weston Street
London SE1
(01 403 4066)

British Institute of
   Management (BIM)
Management House
Parker Street
London WC2B 5PT
(01 405 3456)

Appendix 3

The Newmarket Group and the Provision of Venture Capital

by a director of Newmarket Company (1981) Ltd

Starting your own business is an adventure and Richard Hargreaves' book is a valuable guide to the preparation which is necessary to make a successful beginning. To those who provide the capital, either to support the start-up of new business ventures or to sustain businesses in their early development, the entrepreneur and his business proposal are the man and the plan upon which the decision will be made.

The prior mental exploration of the business and its possible development in the imagination of the entrepreneur can result in a business plan, which not only describes in detail the opportunity, but recognizes the possible hindrances and pitfalls. The plan is therefore able to incorporate the variations which could be adopted to prevent the early failure or serious disablement of the venture. This is useful in demonstrating the potential resilience of the venture and the resourceful planning ability of the entrepreneur. In fact many of the most successful ventures, once started, have diverted from their original plan by responding to new and greater opportunities that occur in the course of their development. Indeed the entrepreneur, who has developed the skill of envisaging his opportunities with a detailed method of exploiting them, can be more successful in that he can rapidly assess such a diversion and adjust his plans with the speed that modern business opportunities often demand.

Venturing in Perspective

A 'venture capitalist' invests in the new for profit. He invests his capital to develop an idea. It is an investment excursion into the unknown with all the risks that can surprise such an exploration. Perhaps the most famous venture

179

capital proposal in history was made by Columbus. He sought capital to venture across the Atlantic in search of a shorter sea route to the Indies. Columbus was the entrepreneur. Luis de Santangel, keeper of Spain's privy purse, was the venture capital manager and Queen Isabella was one of the investors. The venturers on that occasion were rewarded by the 'multiplier', which all venture capital managers like to believe lurks within the ventures they support. The multiplier is the random chance that the reward will exceed expectations by a hundredfold; instead of a sea route you discover the Americas.

The immediate period following the 1939–45 war may not have borne much outward resemblance to fifteenth century Spain, except that a few people foresaw a new world, not geographical but technological. The provision of capital had, of course, been a necessary supplement to ideas which have stimulated thousands of ventures throughout modern history, ventures which have given ever-changing shape and pace to the background of daily life. But it has been in recent times that the speed of physical change has constantly increased as engineering techniques matched the constructions of thought. The war had accelerated scientific and technological developments in jet engines, rocketry, electronics instrumentation, radar, computers and nuclear power, and provided the enormous potential for their further development for peaceful uses. The 'Cold War', however, increased the pressure on the need for continued military advances in technology by the United States. This military requirement has remained a driving force in American technological progress, including the whole space programme and the transistor and solid state circuitry that was essential for its success. It was a technology that would in twenty-five years achieve what still seemed science fiction in 1945 – the landing of a man on the moon.

In the immediate pre-war years in the United States, the best-known private venture capital investors were the very wealthy families of the Rockefellers, Whitneys, Paysons and Burdens. The methods of selecting ventures were hunch and flair modified by financial experience. In the United Kingdom there had been support for ventures from persons with a more eccentric style. In 1931 Lady Houston presented the sum of £100,000 to finance the victorious British entry in the 1931 Schneider Trophy contest, when the British Government refused a subsidy for the Royal Air Force to compete. The development of the Merlin aircraft engine was initially financed by Rolls Royce as a private venture. These acts of philanthropic and far-sighted venture capital support were to prove of inestimable value, for these ventures provided the design for the Spitfire and the engine which powered both the Spitfire and the Hurricane, the fighter aircraft of 1940 upon which Britain's safety was to depend, as well as the Lancaster bomber and the Mosquito.

It was in America in the immediate post-war period that the modern style of venture capital management began. Laurance Rockefeller recognized that the methods which had been used by the military during and after the war, in organizing and managing billions of dollars of research and development programmes, should be applied in the private sector of venture capital to cope with the financing of the new ventures in technology. In addition, he recognized that there was the need to have access to the leading scientific brains, exemplified by the USAF Scientific Advisory Board under Dr Theodore von Karman, which had studied the future of American airpower and guided missiles. It was from this group that Laurance Rockefeller recruited Lt. Colonel Walkowicz, an aeronautical engineer from the Massachussets Institute of Technology. Ted Walkowicz and his colleague Nat Owen, who joined the Whitneys, pioneered venture capital in emerging technologies, a terminology that would have then been unfamiliar. It was not to become popular until the early 1960s, when many of today's leading private venture partnerships in America were formed. Technology by then had become fashionable as the results of its commercial developments became daily more apparent. The professional management styles pioneered by Walkowicz and Owen set the pattern for the new breed of venture capitalists, who contributed personal skills and raised private partnership capital to finance investments. The development of this pattern has reached the stage where in the United States in 1982 the National Venture Capital Association had 130 members with approximately $6 billion in funds for venture investments; in 1981 $1.4 billion of venture capital investments were made in the United States, and Dun & Bradstreet recorded that new business start-ups totalled nearly 600,000 during the year.

Newmarket Group

The Newmarket group was formed in 1972 by three United Kingdom financial institutions, (Equity and Law Life Assurance Society, The Mercantile Investment Trust and Witan Investment Company) and one overseas investment fund (Frobisher Fund N.V.) to carry out a programme of venture capital investment in the United States in co-operation with Venrock Associates, the Rockefeller family venture management team. The London stockbrokers Cazenove & Co. were instrumental in organizing the company and obtaining the permission for the investment overseas of up to $8 million, since exchange controls then regulated all foreign investment from the UK. These institutions, with Cazenove & Co., had previously participated in financing a company in the new North Sea oil and gas exploration venture, which was to succeed as a substantial new British oil exploration and production company, London & Scottish Marine Oil Company (LASMO).

During the 1970s Newmarket's investment policy was exclusively in the United States, since this was a condition of the permission the London institutions had been granted. Despite a period when investment by Newmarket was prevented by the stringency of the exchange control regulations, an initial investment of some US$3.5 million increased in value to approximately US$40 million. In 1979 when UK exchange controls were abolished, plans were made to expand Newmarket's investment programme.

Peter Crisp, who had succeeded Ted Walkowicz on his retirement from Venrock Associates, commented on the flow of new scientific ideas from Britain, particularly in biochemistry and computer software, many of which were later incorporated into American venture capital projects. An example of Anglo-American co-operation in a new industrial venture included Evans & Sutherland Computer Corporation, Newmarket's most rewarding venture investment so far. Evans & Sutherland co-operated with Redifon, a subsidiary of Rediffusion, in providing the computer produced visual image system for the latter's aircraft simulators. The combination has been extremely successful in the world aircraft simulator market. Evans & Sutherland had also co-operated with, and later acquired, Shape Data Limited of Cambridge, a producer of advanced computer aided design programmes. Shape Data was one of the new computer companies which were springing up around Cambridge, deriving their flow of talent from the highly regarded Cambridge University Computer and Engineering Departments. In the light of this activity in new technology, Newmarket decided to form a wholly-owned British subsidiary, Newmarket (Venture Capital) Limited, to invest in ventures in the United Kingdom. At the same time, with King's College, Cambridge, a joint company was formed, New Cambridge Research Company Limited, to encourage and support initial research on scientific ideas which might have commercial application. The Bursar of King's, Michael Cowdy, and the College's investment adviser, Jack Butterworth, responded with enthusiasm to this new venture. In addition, the encouragement and enthusiasm of the late Professor Sir Michael Postan led to Professor Sir Brian Pippard, Cavendish Professor of Physics, and Dr Aaron Klug, who has since been awarded the 1982 Nobel Prize for Chemistry, agreeing to act as scientific advisers to the Newmarket group.

In 1981 the Newmarket group raised $36 million in a public offer of shares in London, the parent company's shares becoming fully listed on the London Stock Exchange; it was the first pure venture capital company to have a listing. At 31st December 1982, Newmarket had net assets worth some US$93 million and had 39 venture investments in the United States and the United Kingdom, plus one in Denmark, one in Canada and one international company in Bermuda. The liquid resources totalled some US$25 million. The group's policy is to concentrate on supporting ventures which are based either on the new application or development of technology or on new scientific developments. Newmarket also seeks to spread the possible public maturities of its investments and therefore will support start-up ventures, new companies in their early development period and companies raising the last tranche of private financing prior to a public listing, provided that the ventures fall within its specified range of criteria.

Newmarket is often described in the press as an investment trust. In the accepted sense of the term it is not. A more accurate description would be a venture capital investment company. While it has similarities to an investment trust in its portfolio spread of ventures and expected maturities, the differences of policy are important. Apart from the higher risks, which are in the nature of its business, the considerable variation in performance of the investments can lead to imbalances in the portfolio, especially where a particularly successful venture can produce a substantial increase in value. Moreover, these imbalances may persist while the particular venture is retained during the continuation of its development.

The group's British subsidiary has an office in the City of London. In New York, co-operation is maintained with Venrock, Ted Walkowicz, who now manages Advanced Technology Ventures, and Cazenove Inc.'s local office. A communication system of Torch microcomputers, developed and manufactured by a British company based in Cambridge which Newmarket (Venture Capital) has backed, now links these offices with offices in Bermuda and Montreal.

The Attitude to Venturing

Although entrepreneurs no longer have the physical challenge of sailing across uncharted oceans in search of new markets, the creation of a new business requires a similar belief and daring to push against the inertia and doubt of the daily routine of life. Whereas entertainers and sportsmen are generally applauded by the press and television, commerce and industry receive sniping commentary. Politicians exhort the creation of new jobs and Trades Unions demand their members' right to work, yet in Britain the solutions to unemployment have involved the extension of the state-owned bureaucratic monoliths that have choked on the restrictions of their own organization. It is a reflection on the publicly-created opinion of our society that the men and women who would create new jobs for their fellow men by their own efforts, receive so little encouragement or regard. Envy of individual success is a warp in the mind of those who declaim the need to help society and yet resent its most able benefactors. But, to the modern entrepreneur these discouragements are the equivalent of the solemn minds that foretold of the everlasting abyss beyond the ocean's far horizon. Entrepreneurial activity is the husbandry of innovation. Innovation is the restless adjustment to the future: stagnation is the satisfied acceptance of the past.

The author of this book has indeed taken his own advice and started a business to advise and assist other ventures in the exciting and arduous task of creating a new business. Newmarket (Venture Capital) has made a venture investment in the author's company to assist in broadening the availability of skilled and experienced help for the creation of new businesses. Venture capital can help to accelerate the new technological developments for the benefit of the economy, society and employment. The managers of such ventures must be able to match the heavy demands that the creation of any new business will place upon them. The present book is a valuable aid to those who would begin their own new business ventures.

The Newmarket Group of Companies

Parent Company
Newmarket Company (1981) Limited
Reid House,
Church Street,
Hamilton 5,
Bermuda

Newmarket (Venture Capital) Limited
57 London Wall,
London EC2M 5TP
(01) 638 4551   Telex 8951549

New Cambridge Research Company Limited
   [Company owned in conjunction with King's College, Cambridge]
57 London Wall,
London EC2M 5TP
(01) 638 4551   Telex 8951549

Newcastle Company Limited
Reid House,
Church Street,
Hamilton 5,
Bermuda

Reading List

Title	Most relevant chapters	Authors	Publisher
Working for Yourself, The Daily Telegraph Guide to Self-Employment	All	Godfrey Golzen	Kogan Page
The Guardian Guide to Running a Small Business	All	Editor: Clive Woodcock	Kogan Page
How to Start and Run Your Own Business	All	M. Mogano	Graham & Trotman
Practical Corporate Planning	3, 11	John Argenti	George Allen & Unwin
Finance for the Non-Accountant	4	L.E. Rockley	Business Books
Managing Your Company's Finances	4, 5, 6, 8, 11	R.L. Hargreaves and R.H. Smith	William Heinemann
Financial and Cost Accounting for Management	4	A.H. Taylor	Macdonald & Evans
Equity and Loan Financing for the Private Company	5, 6	Michael Springman	Gower Press
Money for Business	6	—	Bank of England
Financial Assistance for Industry and Commerce in the United Kingdom	6	—	Peat Marwick Mitchell & Co.
Law for the Small Business	7	Pat Clayton	Kogan Page
Hambro Tax Guide	7	A.S. Silke and W.I. Sinclair	Macdonald Futura
101 Ways of Saving Tax	7	Touche Ross & Co.	Tolleys

Reading List

The Complete Guide to Managing Your Own Business	8, 11	—	Eaglemoss Publications
The Simplex Book-keeping System	8	G. Whitehead	Simplex Advice Bureau, George Vyner Ltd.
The Small Business Book-keeping System	8	—	Foster, Cooper and Company
Control of Working Capital	8	Edited by Margin Gross	Gower Press
Bigger Profits for the the Smaller Firm	8	E.G. Wood	Business Books
A Practical Approach to Financial Management	8	J. Gibbs	Financial Training Publications
How to be Your Own Personnel Manager	8, 11	P. Humphrey	Institute of Personnel Management
Survival Kit for Small Businesses	8, 9	Touche Ross & Co.	Tolleys
Expansion Kit for Business	11	Touche Ross & Co.	Tolleys
Managing the Survival of Smaller Companies	8, 9	S.C. Hazel and	Business Books
The Manager's Guide to Getting the Answers (1980)	Appendix 2	—	Library Association
Use of Management and Business Literature	Appendix 2	K.D.C. Vernon	Butterworths

List of Examples, Check Lists and Forms

Table Number	Title	Page
3.1	Possible Constraints on a New Business Plan	15
3.2	An Example of a List of Guidelines for a Proposed New Business	16
3.3	Some Risks of Starting a New Business and their Possible Consequences	18
3.4	Business Plan Check List	19
3.5	Examples of Possible Objectives for Three Start-ups in the Same Business	22
4.1	The Effect on Profit of Different Depreciation Rates	35
4.2	An Example of a Profit and Loss Account for a Manufacturing Company	37
4.3	The Difference between Cash Flow and Profit	39
4.4	An Example of a Simple Balance Sheet	41
4.5	Important Areas which Need Assumptions when Forecasting	43
4.6	What You Should Consider When Preparing a Sales Forecast	44
4.7	What You Should Consider When Preparing a Production Costs and Gross Profit Forecast	44
4.8	What You Should Consider When Preparing an Overhead Forecast	45
4.9 (Part I)	Profit Forecast for the First Year of Trading of XYZ Ltd	46
4.9 (Part II)	Assumptions for the Profit Forecast of XYZ Ltd for Year One	47

List of Examples

Table Number	Title	Page
4.9 (Part III)	Profit Forecast for the Second Year of Trading of XYZ Ltd	48
4.9 (Part IV)	Assumptions for the Profit Forecast of XYZ Ltd for Year Two	49
4.10	Blank Form for a Profit Forecast	51
4.11	Timing Assumptions Needed for Cash Flow Forecasting	52
4.12 (Part I)	Cash Flow Forecast for the First Year's Trading of XYZ Ltd	53
4.12 (Part II)	Assumptions for the Cash Flow Forecast of XYZ Ltd for Year One	54
4.12 (Part III)	Cash Flow Forecast for the Second Year's Trading of XYZ Ltd	55
4.13	Cash Flow Forecast for 12 Months Ending . . .	56
4.14	A Blank Form for use in Longer Term Cash Flow Projections	57
4.15	Forecast Balance Sheet for XYZ Ltd at the end of the First Year's Trading	58
4.16	Forecast Balance Sheet for XYZ Ltd at the end of the Second Year's Trading	59
5.1	Ways of Reducing Financial Needs	64
5.2	Matching Finance to its uses	67
5.3	Common Types of Finance Available to the Small Business	70
5.4	Possible Ways of Raising Money Yourself	73
6.1	A Guide to Development and Venture Capital Facilities	76
6.2	What to Include in Your Application for Finance	89
7.1	Partnership Versus Limited Company	99
7.2	Partnership Agreement Check List	101
7.3	A summary of the Legal Position of Directors	102
7.4	Statutory Accounting Requirements	105
7.5	Expenses which can be Deducted in Calculating Taxable Profit and Allowances which can be claimed by a Sole Trader or Partnership	107
7.6	Expenses which can be Deducted in Calculating Taxable Profit and Allowances which can be claimed by a Company	110
7.7	Formal Registration Requirements	112
7.8	Insurances to Consider	113
7.9	Points to Remember when Employing People	113

Table Number	*Title*	*Page*
7.10	An Example of a Possible Form for use as a Written Statement under the Employment Protection (consolidation) Act 1978	117
8.1	The Minimum Information the Management Needs	120
8.2	An Example of an Order Position Summary	123
8.3	A comparison of the Forecast Cash Position for a Particular Period with Achievement	126
8.4	The Stages Needed for a Full Budgetary Control System	129
8.5	An Example of a Company's Overhead Expenses Allocated to Specific Managers for Budgetary Control Purposes	130
8.6	An Example of a Profit and Loss Account showing the Contribution to Profit from separate Products	133
8.7	Control Points for an Invoice Credit System	134
8.8	A For for an Aged Debtor Report	135
8.9	Control Points for a Purhasing System	136
8.10	Check List for a Review of the Cash Needs of Your Business	138
9.1	Factors which affect Success and Failure	145

Index

Accountants, 152
Accounting records, 120–1
Advisers, 5, 90, 151
Applications for finance, 91
Articles of Association, 100

Balance sheet, 38, 41
Breakeven, 58
Budgetary control, 127–32
Business contacts, 151
Business plan, 147–9

Cash flow, 38
Cash flow forecasting, see Forecasting,
    Forecasts
Cash crisis, surviving a, 63–6, 137–41
Competition, 25
Consultants, 155
Contingency, 61
Convertible loan, 69
Cost information, 124–5
Costs
    fixed, 123
    variable, 42, 123
Credit, 33, 38
Credit control, 132–7
Credit factoring, 68, 70, 90
Customers, 26
Current assets, 32, 39, 64–6
Current liabilities, 40, 64

Debentures, 68, 90
Depreciation, 35
Directors, legal position of, 102–3

Employees, 112–8, see also People
Employment contract, 117–8
Equity, 72, 91

Financial structure, 66
Fixed assets, 32, 39, 63–4
Forecasting
    assumptions, 40, 43, 47, 49–50, 52, 54, 61
    balance sheets, 55, 58–9
    cash flow, 50, 53–7
    gross profit, 42–4
    overheads, 43–5
    production costs, 42–4
    sales, 42–3, 46
Forecasts, 40–62, 122, 124, 128, 130
    phased, 60

Government aid, 154

Hire purchase, 65, 71, 90

Incorporation, 98, 100
Insurances, 113
Invoice discounting, 70

Leasing, 65, 71, 90
Licensing, 27
Limited company, 97
Long-term finance, 67, 69, 71

Management accounts, 131, 133
Market, 13, 24
Market niche, 13
Matching, 66–7
Medium-term finance, 67–8, 71
Memorandum of Association, 100

National Insurance, 97, 109

Objectives, 21
Order position, 122–3, 127
Ordinary shares, 72, 91
Overdraft, 68, 93
Overheads, 36, 66

Index

forecasting, *see* Forecasting, Forecasts
Overhead lead, 60, 63–4

Partnership, 97, 100
Patents, 26–7
People, 31, 112–8, 141–3, 146, 148, 157–9
Permanent capital, 67, 71
Personal guarantee, 18, 73
Phased forecasts, 60
Plant and equipment, 31, 63–4
Preference shares, 69, 72
Premises, 30, 65
Pricing, 28
Production, 27
Products, 26
Profit, 35
Profit and loss account, 36–7
Profit forecasts, *see* Forecasting, Forecasts

Registration, formal, 109, 111
Research and development costs, 36

Risks, 3, 5, 17–18

Sensitivity, 61
Share capital, 71–2, 91
Shareholders' funds, 40
Short-term finance, 67–8, 70
Sole trader, 96
Solicitors, 153
Sources of finance, 76
Statutory accounting requirements, 105
Stock position, 126
Subcontracting, 28
Suppliers, 29

Tax, 36, 39, 104
    limited company, 98, 108–111
    partnership, 98, 106–8

Unique selling edge, 13
Unlimited liability, 96

Working capital, 32